CULTURAL Accents

Ronke Luke-Boone

Published by

kp **krause publications**
An F&W Publications Company

To place an order or obtain a free catalog,
please call (800) 258-0929.

All photographs, unless otherwise noted, are by Kim Johnson.
Edited by Christine Townsend
Designed by Sharon Laufenberg and Mary Lou Marshall

Library of Congress Catalog Number 2003108200
ISBN 0-87349-601-9

Printed in China

"The future belongs to those who believe in the beauty of their dreams."

–Eleanor Roosevelt

Acknowledgments

I loved writing this book. It was a great platform to share my conviction that traditional arts and crafts of diverse cultures are relevant to our modern lives. While I am certainly not an expert in cultural anthropology, I am fascinated by the role of arts and crafts in all societies. With this book, I hope to share with you great ideas for ways to utilize traditional designs in your busy, contemporary life. Beyond that, I hope I inspire you to take a second look at the arts, crafts, and other traditions of cultures from around the world.

Many people contributed to turning my original ideas into reality. I thank God for the opportunities He offers me. I am always amazed at how He opens doors. My ability to do anything comes through Him.

I owe a big "Thank you" to my parents and family who encourage (and humor!) my every bright idea in pursuit of crafts.

Thanks to everyone at Krause—including Christine Townsend, Julie Stephani, and Paul Kennedy-for embracing my ideas and bringing this book to fruition.

Thanks to Kim Johnson and Jefry Wright from Urban Oasis Studio for photography. Once again, you were great to work with. Bijan, Mehrdad, and Mack from McLean Photo—as usual, you were great, thank you. Thank you Trina, for being a gracious model, and thanks Samantha for make-up. I thank Mark Wagner, Carine Fabius, and Lisa Butterworth for so graciously contributing photos, diagrams, and additional information.

"Life is a great big canvas; throw all the paint on it you can."

–Danny Kaye

Table of Contents

Introduction 6

Using this Book 7

Chapter 1

Getting Started Stenciling and Stamping 8

Cutting Stencils 9

Stenciling 12

Cutting Stamps 16

How to Stamp 18

Stamping Versus Stenciling-
When to Choose Which 21

Chapter 2

Spice Tones around the World 22

Aztec-Inca-Maya Director's Chair 23

Australian Aboriginal Wall Hanging
. 25

African Safari Wall Hanging . . .27

Tulip Patch 29

Kuba Cloth Footstool 33

Rock Painting Wall Art 34

Aztec Drinking Glass 36

Adinkra Coasters 37

Kente Wall Panel 39

Mudcloth Mirror 40

Australian Aboriginal Flower Pot .42

Mountain Sheep Flower Pot 43

Hopi Gold Leaf Cactus Planter . .44

Mehndi-Henna Bed Linen 45

Feather Silk Pillows 47

Linen and Brocade Throw 49

Paper-covered Lampshade 50

Chapter 3

Cool Blues with a Hint of Red 52

Adire Director's Chair 53

Hopi-patterned Plate 55

Moroccan Tile Plate 57

Blue Aztec Drinking Glass 58

Adire Coasters 59

Silver Leaf Votive 60

Beaded Napkin Rings 61

Henna Mehndi Napkins 62

Asian Inspired Hot Plate 63

Sashiko Glass Container 65

Kuba Cloth Patterned Container .67

Etched Adire Wall Art 69

Mondrian Inspired Mirror 70

Mondrian Inspired Hot Plate 72

Paper-covered Gift Boxes 73

Painted Ceramic Door and Drawer
Pulls .74

Wall Pictures from Notecards . . .75

Chapter 4

Natural Textures 76

Wooden Table Runner 77

Gold Leaf Vase 78

Adinkra Place Mats 79

Raffia Napkin Rings 80

Hopi Pattern Bowl 81

Apache Basket Weave Bowl 82

Chapter 5

Asian Accents 83

Bamboo Place Mats 84

Chinese Decoupage Planter 86

Shoji Votive Lantern 87

Chinese Calligraphy Votive 89

Chinese Peace and Good Luck Tiles 90

Chapter 6

Pretty Powder Room . . .92

Arabic Ceramic Tiles 93

Handmade Soap 95

Adinkra Towels 96

Paisley Bottle 97

Chapter 7

Around the World
While You Work 98

Moroccan Tile Cork Board 99

Indian Spice Paisley Notebook . .100

Seminole Lampshade 102

Handmade Thai-paper Box 105

Nepalese-Tibetan Paper-covered
Magazine Holders 106

Raffia-wrapped Clay Pot 107

Chapter 8

Words of Wisdom 108

Personal Stationery 110

Italian Gilded Tile 111

Pillow Talk-Embroidered Silk Pillows 112

Chapter 9

Clothing 116

Mehndi Silk Chiffon Blouse . . .117

Nomad Coat-Fusion of Cultures 117

Linen Kuba-patterned Outfit . . .118

Ibo Water Spirit Dress 119

Linen and Korhogo Jacket 120

Indian Summer Sheath 121

Mehndi Linen Blouse 122

Mudcloth T-shirt 122

Bibliography 123

Resources 125

Index 126

Introduction

I t has become a cliché to say that we live in a global village. Indeed, exotic places that were once far-flung are now no further than a mouse-click away for us "armchair" travelers, and a plane trip or two for the real globe-trotters. Modern technology may have shrunk geographic distance, yet it is our differences and unique characteristics that make us interesting to each other. Yes, global trade has brought McDonalds® restaurants to Mumbai and Cairo, but most travelers don't go to India or Egypt in search of hamburgers. When we visit new places, we are interested in experiencing the peoples and cultures of that place through the food and drink, arts and crafts, ornaments and textiles, decorative traditions, aesthetics, literature and song, dress, mythology and rituals, and on and on. Yet, these traditions do not exist in isolation from global trade and technology. The Internet offers artisans in remote communities a marketplace through which they can offer their products to the world around the clock.

Each culture embraces and incorporates global influences in its own unique way. Tulips, for example, which most people think of as being synonymous with the Netherlands, were actually native to Asia. The paisley, which is perceived as originally British, emerged from the British desire to replicate the fine shawls woven in Kashmir.

I am fascinated by the arts and crafts traditions of cultures around the world. Learning how these traditions emerged, their roles within a culture and how they are practiced, is a window onto a world different from mine. In this book-Cultural Accents—I share projects that are inspired by or capture the crafts, techniques, or designs of cultures around the world. You'll see beautiful glass containers decorated with Sashiko quilting and Kuba cloth patterns, vibrant silk pillows sporting big bunches of tulips, a wall hanging decorated with Australian Aboriginal motifs, and a silk chiffon blouse decorated with Mehndi motifs. These are all contemporary items that fit perfectly into our modern lives.

I hope that this book inspires you to seek more information about the peoples and cultures that the projects reflect. I also hope you embrace the Japanese concept of Mingei ("folk art," or the art of common people) and continue to support artisans around the world who make wonderful handmade artifacts that reflect their cultures.

Using this Book

This book is, first and foremost, a crafts book. It offers projects for all levels of home décor and personal fashion. The projects are inspired by cultures from many peoples of our globe-Chinese, Australia's Aborigines, the Hopis and Seminoles of the United States, the Dutch, the Aztecs, Incas, and Mayans of North and Central America, the Kubas, Senufos, and Ashantis from Africa, to name a few. Try out these projects. Feel free to modify them as you wish to make them your own.

In addition, I include background information on many of the cultures that inspired the projects. Please read these little text boxes as you make the projects and browse through this book. I hope these tidbits give you a first connection to the people and their cultures. If you like what you see, I encourage you to do your own research on them ... I'm sure that you'll come away fascinated and enriched. I hope this book offers you a peek into how traditional arts, crafts, and artifacts can be translated into our busy contemporary lives.

Ronke
www.rlboone.com
Ronke@rlboone.com

1 | Getting Started
Stenciling and Stamping

Stenciling and stamping are fun, easy ways to personalize projects. You can create a single pattern or repeat a pattern over the entire surface of your project, or you can limit yourself to borders or trims. Use stencils and stamps to decorate your projects, or personalize purchased products such as napkins, plates, curtains, or clothing.

There are many commercially available stencils and stamps from which to choose. Craft stores and mail order resources offer everything from basic flowers to wonderful cultural images. Can't find what you want from this vast selection? Don't worry. Simply make your own stencils and stamps using basic supplies from a craft or office supply store. Pictures, photographs, and nature are great sources of ideas, and there are many sources for copyright-free designs. Creating your own stencils and stamps is simple and, with a little practice, you'll be making lots of them.

In this section, we go over the basic supplies and techniques you'll need to make your own stencils and stamps.

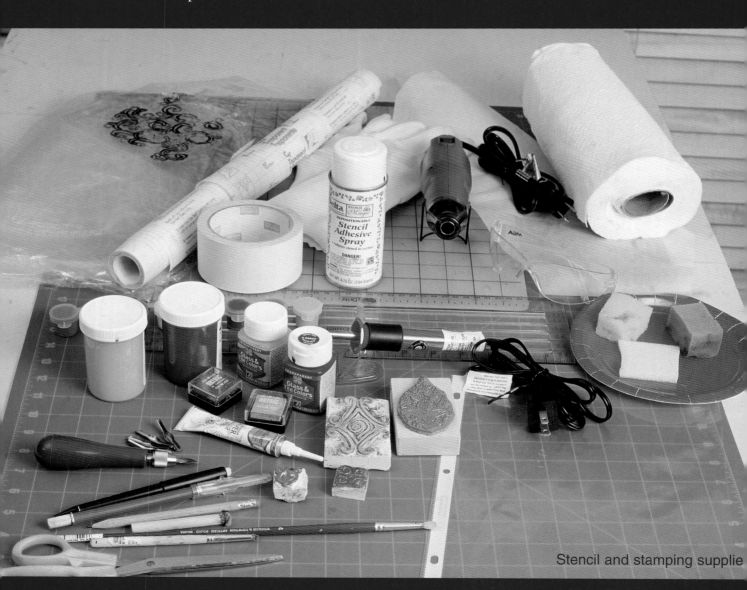

Stencil and stamping supplie

Cutting Stencils

The following instructions are for making stencils with a craft knife or a stencil burner and overhead transparencies or document protectors. If you are using a stencil burner instead of a craft knife, replace the rotary cutting mat with clear glass (use the glass from a picture frame).

Materials

- ☐ Blank paper
- ☐ Pen or pencil
- ☐ Masking tape
- ☐ A picture or design (you can draw your own design)
- ☐ Craft knife (X-Acto® knife)
- ☐ Overhead transparencies, document protectors, stencil plastic or Contact® paper
- ☐ Rotary cutting mat (or cardboard or old magazine to use as a cutting surface)

If using stencil burner, instead of a craft knife you will need:

- ☐ Stencil burner
- ☐ Clear glass

Instructions

Draw your design on a blank sheet of paper. (Or, photocopy the picture you want to use in your stencil. If you are making a project for re-sale, be sure you adhere to copyright requirements.) In the picture below, you can see both the original picture of tulips and the line tracing. You do not have to trace a line diagram of your picture before you cut a stencil. I show both so you can see your options.

Note: the larger the image, the easier it is to cut a stencil.

Stencil supplies and picture of tulips.

Cutting Stencils

Setting Up to Use an X-Acto® Knife

Tape the piece of paper with your image to your cutting mat with masking tape. Position and tape the overhead transparency over the image so that there is at least 3" around the image.

Cutting stencil with an X-Acto® knife.

Setting Up to Use a Stencil Burner

Review manufacturers' instructions for using a stencil burner. Tape your image onto your work surface. Position the glass over the image. Place your stencil vinyl over the glass and tape in place. You should be able to see the image through all the layers.

Cutting stencil with a stencil burner.

Cutting Stencils

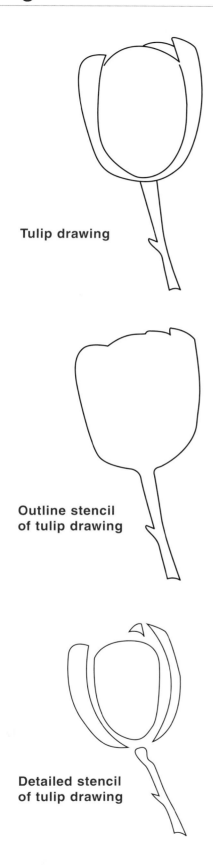

Tulip drawing

**Outline stencil
of tulip drawing**

**Detailed stencil
of tulip drawing**

Tips for Cutting Outline Shape Stencils

Cutting outline shapes are the easiest stencils you can make. However, outline stencils do not give dimension and depth details in your image; instead, you will create a flat image. This effect is sometimes sufficient if the outline of an image conveys the effect you want. To cut a stencil that gives you an outline, simply cut the plastic around the outlines of the image. The plastic will fall away leaving a shaped stencil.

Tips for Cutting Stencils with Depth and Dimension

Stencils with depth and dimension are always more interesting. These stencils give a more realistic impression of your object. To create stencils that reflect realistic images, do not simply cut around the edges of your image. Instead, where two sections of the image come together, you will need to cut out each section so that a portion of stencil plastic forms a bridge between the stencil areas and the remaining plastic. See the illustrations on the left. With a bit of practice, you will be able to cut these stencils easily.

Stenciling

Once you have your stencil, it's very easy to decorate a project. Here's a basic primer on stenciling. Important: Practice the following techniques on scrap (fabric, paper, or wood) surfaces first before using it on your project!

Materials

- ❏ Project or surface to be decorated (fabric, wood, paper, etc.)
- ❏ Stencil
- ❏ Ink or paint (appropriate for project surface)
- ❏ Sponges (one for each color if you don't want to mix paint)
- ❏ Stencil brush with short, stiff bristles
- ❏ Palette to mix paint (paper plate or plastic container cover are suitable)
- ❏ Masking tape
- ❏ Stencil spray adhesive
- ❏ Bowl of water for rinsing
- ❏ Plastic sheeting

Instructions

1 Tape plastic sheeting over your work surface. Place your project surface (fabric, wood, paper, etc.) on the plastic. Tape fabric or paper taut onto the plastic surface (using weights is optional). Hold flat, thin wood in place with weights.

2 Secure the stencil over your project surface using stencil spray adhesive or masking tape.

3 Use brush to place a small portion of paint on your palette. Rinse brush.

4 Dip your sponge or brush lightly into the paint to "load" your implement. You only want a little paint on your sponge or brush.

5 Using quick up and down hand movements—raising and lowing at wrist—fill the stencil space. Continue to load and fill the stencil space until complete. Note: The best results are achieved when you use paint sparingly.

6 Allow project to dry. Follow manufacturers' instructions to set paint, if necessary.

7 Clean your stencil, sponge, and/or brush by rinsing in water. Dry with paper towel, or allow to dry on draining board.

Stencil brush lightly loaded with paint. Stencil held in place with masking tape and weight.

Stenciling tulips.

Experiment!

Now you know the basics, it's time to experiment to get more stunning effects and results. Try some of the following techniques.

Combining Colors

Combine colors in one stencil to further enhance texture. Fill in the space with one color. Go back over the space with a darker color to enhance edges. Or, fill in the space with streaks or accents of other colors to add texture.

In the image above right, the tulips are stenciled in one color—a bright, sunny yellow. The tulips are pretty, but look flat.

To add depth and character after the paint dried, I added light touches of dark red over the yellow paint in random places. The dark red touches enliven the tulips. They no longer look flat.

Tulip stenciled in one color.

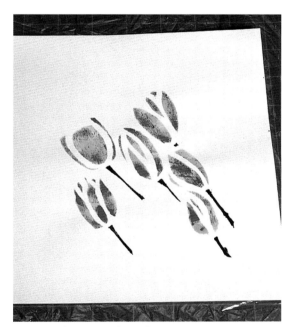

Tulip stenciled in two colors to add depth.

Stenciling

Combining Stencils

Combine several stencils. For example, use simple shapes such as circles or squares as a background, and then stencil an interesting shape over the background stencil.

I created the pattern (shown below) of a grid on squares by combining two stencils—one of large squares, with another of small squares.

Here's how to do it. First stencil the large squares in a lighter color. I used silvery blue. Note: Weights hold the stencil in place. You can use masking tape or stencil spray adhesive if you prefer.

Once the large square pattern is completed, allow it to dry.

Next, position the small square pattern stencil over the large silver square and stencil the pattern with dark blue paint. If the stencil will overlap the area previously stenciled, allow the paint to dry before stenciling over the next area.

Try this technique with other shapes. Experiment and see what you get.

Create shadows of one stencil by using two paints—one dark and one light

Here's how to do it. First stenciling your image with the lighter color. Allow to dry.

Next shift the stencil slightly off to one side of the original print and stencil the darker image. For the second layer of darker squares, I shifted the stencil slightly downwards and over to the right. Use paint sparingly.

Try alternating the darker and lighter stencil and see how the image changes.

Grid on square stenciled pattern.

Stenciling large squares.

Stenciling

Large square base pattern.

Stenciling small squares over
the large squares.

Squares shadowing and
floating over each other.

Stenciling squares in lighter color.

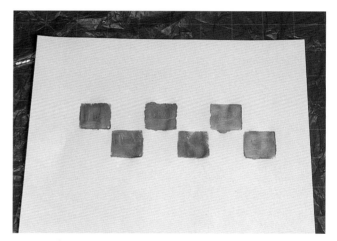

Squares stenciled in lighter color.

Darker squares stenciled over lighter color.

Cutting Stamps

Stamping is fun, and cutting your own stamps is easy—remember potato stamping when you were a child?

The following instructions show how to make stamps from erasers and eraser blocks. But you can use other materials for making stamps: potatoes, high density foam, sponges, linoleum, rubber blocks, and computer mouse pads are all suitable for stamping, and each will give you a different effect . . . so experiment.

Made and purchased stamps.

Stamp blanks—eraser and cutting blocks.

Materials

- ❑ Erasers or eraser block (I often use Staedler®)
- ❑ Linoleum cutting tools
- ❑ Tracing paper
- ❑ Pencil (soft lead)
- ❑ Pen
- ❑ Picture (to transfer to stamp)
- ❑ Masking tape

Cutting Stamps

Instructions

1 Trace picture to tracing paper. Outline the image in pen. Repeat the pen outline several times until you have a dark line.

2 Place the tracing paper, pen line down, onto the rubber block. Ensure that there is some rubber block around the pen lines. Holding the tracing paper in place with one hand, use your pencil to shade the surface of the tracing paper. Cover all the pen lines. By doing this, you will transfer the outline of your image onto the rubber stamp.

3 With linoleum cutting tools, trim away the area of the rubber stamp that is undesired, leaving the raised area of the image for stamping.

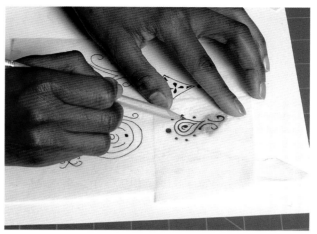

Tracing the image.

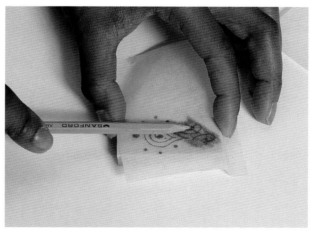

Shade back of tracing paper to transfer image to eraser.

Image transferred to eraser.

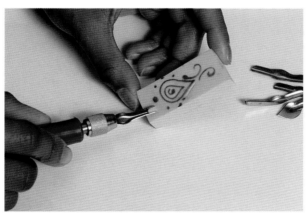

Cutting away eraser around lines to create raised image for stamping.

Stamp of image.

How to Stamp

Stamping supplies.

*I*mportant: *Practice the following techniques on scrap materials first before using them on your project!*

Materials

- ☐ Project or surface to be decorated (fabric, wood, paper, etc.)
- ☐ Stamps
- ☐ Ink pad or paint (appropriate for project surface)
- ☐ Bowl of water for rinsing
- ☐ Plastic sheeting

Applying paint to stamp using a sponge.

Applying paint to stamp using paint pad.

Stamping image onto surface.

Two stamps and two colors to create project.

Instructions

1 Tape plastic sheeting over your work surface. Place your project surface (fabric, wood, paper, etc.) on the plastic. Tape fabric or paper taut onto work surface. You can use weights to hold flat, thin wood in place.

2 If you are using paint, use a paintbrush to place a small portion of paint on your palette. Rinse the brush. Dip your sponge or brush lightly into the paint to load your implement. Cover the stamp completely with paint. Be careful to only place paint on raised areas of your stamp. If you are using a paint pad, press your stamp firmly onto the pad. Do not rock the stamp.

3 Press stamp onto surface for decoration. Be careful not to rock the stamp as this will smudge the image. Continue stamping until your project is complete. Combine multiple stamps and colors in one project, if you wish.

4 Allow the project to dry. Follow manufacturers' instructions to set paint, if necessary.

5 Clean your stamp, sponge, and brush with soap and water. Allow them to dry.

How to Stamp

Experiment!

Now that you know the basics, it's time to experiment to get more stunning effects and results; try some of the following techniques.

Combining Colors

Combine colors on one stamp to further enhance texture. Ink stamp all over with base color. Then apply second color to selective areas of the stamp of your choosing. Work quickly so that ink does not dry.

Immediately press stamp onto decorative surface.

Bronze ink being applied to upper portion of a stamp previously pressed onto red ink pad.

Combining Stamps

Combine several stamps. For example, use simple shapes, such as circles or squares as a background, and then stamp an interesting shape over the background. The pattern below was created by stamping two patterns randomly, using three paints and partially overlapping some stamps.

Apply ink to stamp. Stamp onto surface for decoration. Continue stamping patterns in varying colors, overlapping some patterns.

Stamp applied to decorative surface

Applying ink to stamp.

Continue stamping in varying colors, overlapping patterns until you are happy with the results.

Two-tone stamp of Chinese calligraphy

How to Stamp

Embossing with Powder

Embossing stamps with embossing powders is a great technique to add depth and richness to a project. You will need an embossing heat tool, available at craft stores, to do this.

Apply ink to stamp. Stamp onto surface for decoration.

Immediately pour embos-sing powder over wet stamp. Ensure stamp is completely covered with powder. You may also choose to sprinkle emboss-ing powder over image instead of pouring.

Carefully lift up project and pour excess embossing powder back into container.

Following manufacturer's instructions, heat the embossing powder with your heating tool to set. Be careful, as the instrument can get very hot.

See the difference embossing can make to a stamp? The motif on the right (see page 21) is embossed with powder, the one on the left is not.

Embossing powder poured over wet stamp.

Pouring excess embossing powder back into container.

How to Stamp

Embossing stamp.

Embossing makes a difference. Right-hand motif is embossed. Left is not.

Stamping Versus Stenciling – When to Choose Which

You can use either stamping or stenciling to decorate your project. Here are some basic guidelines to determine whether to use a stamp or a stencil.

Type of Image	Stenciling	Stamping
Small Image	Stenciling is appropriate. Cutting out the small details may require practice and patience.	Stamping is appropriate. Cutting out the small details may require practice and patience.
Large Image	Be careful not to cut out large sections as that could weaken the stencil.	Limited by the size of the block you can cut and conveniently handle at your work area.
Complicated Design	You may have to make multiple stencils to complete one image.	You may need to practice cutting complicated patterns on separate blocks before cutting your final block.

2 | Spice Tones
Around the World

The rich tones of red, browns, greens, golds, and ochres featured in these wonderful accessories are sure to add warmth to any space.

A mix of spice-toned accessories.

Aztec-Inca-Maya Director's Chair

This striking director's chair is inspired by the designs and aesthetics of the Aztecs, Incas, and Mayans, three great civilizations of our ancient world. The golden yellow canvas, the circular stencil, and the patterns in the stencil are all adaptations of elements of these noble cultures. This chair makes a cheerful seating addition.

Skilled Metal Artisans

The Aztecs, Incas, and Mayans were skilled metal artisans. Precious metals such as gold, silver, and platinum were important in all three civilizations. Aztec goldsmiths enjoyed high status within society. Artisans of all three civilizations made stunning jewelry and ceremonial artifacts out of precious metals. Ornate curved, curled, and linear elements were used to decorate many of these artifacts.

Aztec director's chair.

Keeping Track of Time

Precisely measuring time was important in the Aztec civilization. Many rituals had to be performed at specific times, so an accurate calendar was necessary. The Aztec calendar was divided into eighteen months of twenty days. A picture of the calendar shows that it was round, with very detailed carvings of the sun at the center and ornate patterns to mark divisions of time and important cycles in circular bands around the center.

The patterns, shape, and details of the Aztec calendar and Aztec, Inca, and Maya gold work are the inspiration for the stencil used to make the director's chair.

Aztec-Inca-Maya Director's Chair

Materials

- ☐ Director's chair seat covering
- ☐ Acrylic paints:
  Gold
  Bronze
  Red
- ☐ Plastic dish or paper plate
- ☐ Stencil brush and sponges
- ☐ Stencil spray
- ☐ Plastic sheeting
- ☐ Weights (or soup cans)
- ☐ Masking tape (optional)
- ☐ Pencil
- ☐ Ruler or tape measure
- ☐ Stencil making supplies
  (see page 9)
- ☐ Rubber gloves
- ☐ Plastic sheeting
- ☐ Additional supplies for setting
  paint according to manufac-
  turers instructions

Instructions

This project is suitable for all skill levels.

1 Make stencil following guidelines (see page 9).

2 Cover work surface with plastic sheeting.

3 Using tape measure and pencil, mark the center of the chair seat and back.

4 Place the chair seat on sheeting. You may place weights at the corners to hold in it place (you may also use masking tape).

5 Place a small amount of paints on your paint dish. Stencil one half of the seat, blending paints to make pleasing colors as you work. Allow the first half to dry.

6 Stencil the chair back in the same way. Allow it to dry.

7 Complete stenciling the other half of the chair seat. Allow it to dry.

8 Follow manufacturer's instructions for setting the paint.

Enlarge stencil by 128%

Australian Aboriginal Wall Hanging

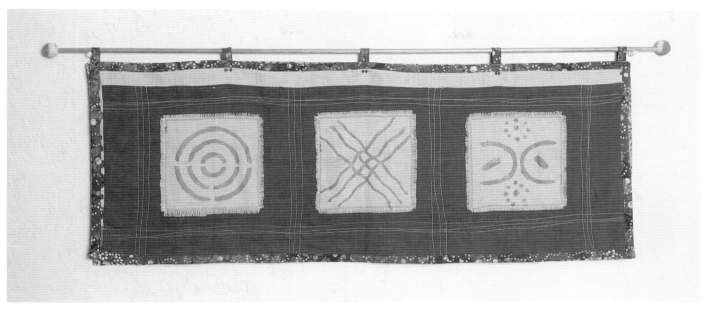

Wall hanging with Australian Aboriginal symbols.

T his simple, yet striking wall hanging uses common *Australian Aboriginal symbols to project a very modern graphic image that will look great on any wall in your home.*

Aboriginal Symbols

Art is an important element of Australian Aboriginal life. Aborigines created art exclusively for traditional and ceremonial uses. Today, their art is created not only for traditional purposes, but also in response to commercial demand for these expressive pieces. Australian Aboriginal art has enjoyed a wonderful following among art collectors in the last 30 years. The dot paintings are the most famous, but other art styles are enjoying strong appreciation.

The contemporary art form that we admire today, and call "Australian Aboriginal Art" is a vital link to one of the world's oldest cultures. Contemporary art uses the same basic set of symbols, such as dots, circles, half-circles, straight and curved lines that have been used in traditional ceremonies for centuries. Each set of symbols can have various meanings depending on the context. Concentric circles typically mean campsites or watering holes. "U" shapes represent people sitting. Straight lines next to U's depict domestic implements or tools. Wavy lines depict water, rain, or smoke. Artists can tell elaborate stories by combining many symbols together.

Materials

- ☐ Red linen, ¾ yd
- ☐ Dark yellow linen, ½ yd
- ☐ ½" wide bias, 2½ yd
- ☐ Matching thread
- ☐ Bronze acrylic paint
- ☐ Stencil brush or sponge
- ☐ Batting, ½ yd
- ☐ Iron
- ☐ Sewing pins
- ☐ Sewing machine
- ☐ Stencil making supplies (see page 9)
- ☐ Rubber gloves

Australian Aboriginal Wall Hanging

Instructions

This project is suitable for all skill levels.

1 **Out of red linen:**
Cut one piece 12" x 32" (label A)
Cut one piece 10¾" x 32" (label B)
Cut one piece 2" x 32" (label C)

Out of yellow linen:
Cut one piece 1¾" x 32" (label D)
Cut three pieces 6" x 6" (label E)

Out of batting:
Cut one piece 12" x 32"

2 With right sides together, stitch B to D along the 32" side with ¼" seam. Press seam open.

3 Cut stencils of desired Aboriginal motifs.

4 Mark center point of each E piece.

5 Stencil a motif on each E piece. Allow to dry. Follow manufacturer's instructions for setting stencil paint as necessary.

6 From the center point of each piece E, position, and pin each stenciled square on the joined piece from Step 2 as follows:

7 Stitch each stenciled square in place by zigzag stitching ½" from the edge.

8 Pin batting to the back of the wall hanging and stitch above, below, and between each stenciled panel. Press.

9 Baste A to the back of the front panel.

10 Encase the raw edges of the wall hanging in bias binding. Pin and stitch bias in place finishing the raw edges of the wall hanging.

11 To make loops, fold piece C in half along the length. Press. Fold again in half along and press. You will have a ½" wide piece. Cut five 4" long pieces. Fold each piece in half to make loops. Position each loop evenly along the top edge of wall hanging and stitch in place.

Aboriginal art symbols are inspired by the ancestral symbols from the Dreaming, upon which Aboriginal religious life centers. The Dreaming has nothing to do with dreams or unreality. Instead it describes the natural, spiritual and moral order of the universe. During the Dream Time ancestors traveled throughout the country creating rivers, rocks, water holes, hills and the land. In fact, the Dreaming spans all time — from creation of the universe to a time beyond living memory — and offers a guide to living that Australian Aborigines celebrate and adhere to today. (Sources: Aboriginal Art, Wally Caruana, Thames & Hudson, New York, 1993, http://www.aboriginalarton-line.com, http://www.aboriginalaustralia.com)

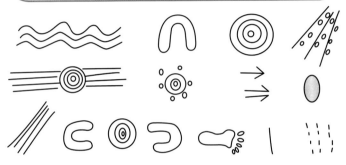

Aboriginal symbols.

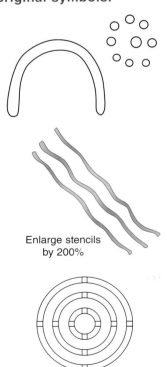

Enlarge stencils
by 200%

African Safari Wall Hanging

African safari wall hanging.

The African safari embodies visions of an exotic vacation. Being able to spend unhurried time surrounded by nature is a pleasure many of us would opt for if we had the chance. So, bring some of that wonderful imagery into your home with this wonderful African safari wall hanging. I used stamps from Rubber Stampede®. You may use other animal stamps or stencils available at your crafts store.

Materials

- ❑ Dark yellow linen, 1 yd
- ❑ Batik 1, ½ yd
- ❑ Batik 2, ¼ yd
- ❑ Batik 3, 1 yd
- ❑ Batting, ½ yd
- ❑ ½" wide bias, 3½ yd
- ❑ Stamps:
  - Giraffe
  - Monkey
  - Tiger
  - Grass
  - Foliage
- ❑ Matching thread
- ❑ Acrylic paints:
  - Medium brown
  - Light brown
  - Dark orange
  - Dark green
  - Light green
- ❑ Iron
- ❑ Sewing machine
- ❑ Sewing pins
- ❑ Rubber gloves

Instructions

This project requires basic sewing skills.

1 **Out of yellow linen:**
Cut one piece 7³/₄" x 9³/₄" (label A)
Cut one piece 9¹/₂" x 9¹/₄" (label B)
Cut one piece 5¹/₄" x 9¹/₄" (label C)

Out of Batik 1, cut:
One piece 2¹/₂" x 9¹/₄" (label D)
Two pieces 2" x 12¹/₄" (label H)
Two pieces 2" x 29¹/₂" (label I)

Out of Batik 2, cut:
One piece 9³/₄" x 2" (label E)
One piece 1¹/₂" x 9¹/₄" (label F)

Out of Batik 3, cut:
Three pieces 1¹/₂" x 9¹/₄" (label G)
One piece 2" x 32" (label J)

Cut bias to make bias binding (optional)

2 **Stamp:**
■ Monkey and foliage on piece A
■ Giraffe and grass on piece B
■ Tiger and grass on piece C
■ Allow to dry. Follow manufacturer's instructions for setting stencil paint.

3 **With ¼" seam, join the following pieces together:**
■ Piece E to the bottom of piece A to complete the "Monkey Panel"

■ Piece G to the bottom of piece C
■ Piece F to the top of piece C
■ Piece D to the top of piece F to complete the "Tiger Panel"

Finished lengths are shown for the three panels. Join the Giraffe panel (piece B) to the Tiger and Monkey panels using the remaining G pieces. Press each seam open after stitching.

4 With ¼" seam, join piece I to the top and bottom of the center panel. Join piece H to each short edge to complete "framing" the front panel. Press each seam open after stitching.

5 Out of batting, cut a piece to fit the underside of the front panel. Pin and baste batting to back of front panel. Stitch front to batting in areas of your choice to secure the layers together. You may stitch panels together by stitching squares of triangles.

6 Encase the raw edges of the wall hanging in bias binding. Pin and stitch bias in place finishing the raw edges of the wall hanging.

7 To make loops, fold piece J in half along the length. Press. Fold again in half along and press. You will have a ¹/₂" wide piece. Cut five 4" long pieces. Fold each piece in half to make loops. Position each loop evenly along the top edge of the wall hanging and stitch in place.

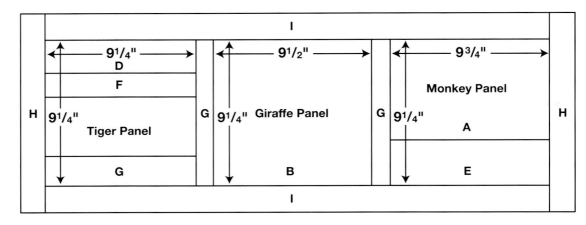

African Safari Panel.

Tulip Patch

love these pillows — they are among my favorites that I've made. Bunches of tulips on big bursts of color say it's spring. They're a wonderful way to add spark to your living room or bedroom!

Tulip Patch silk pillows.

Tulips: The Dutch Symbol with Asian Roots

Like many, you've probably always believed tulips are from the Netherlands. The tulips you get from your florist are probably grown in Holland—the Dutch plant three billion tulip bulbs every year, approximately two billion of which they export. While the flower is synonymous with things Dutch, tulips originally hailed from mountainous regions in central Asia. Their primary genetic center is near the capital of Pakistan, Islamabad, from where they spread east to China, Mongolia, and beyond. From a second genetic center in Azerbaijan and Armenia, tulips spread to Europe.

Interestingly, most people in the Netherlands think tulips originally came from Turkey. This is because when tulips were first introduced into Europe in the 1500s, these regions belonged to the great Ottoman Empire, also known as the Turkish Empire or Persia. The Turks were known to cultivate tulips as early as A.D. 1000.

Tulips came to the Netherlands about 410 years ago. Carolus Clusius (1526-1609), head botanist at the University of Leiden, planted the first tulips in the Netherlands in 1593. A renowned botanist, Clusius worked in Prague and Vienna. Among the many plants he cultivated were the tulips that were given to him by De Busbecq. De Busbecq was the ambassador to the court of Sultan Suleiman in Constantinople, the seat of the Ottoman Empire. It was there that De Busbecq encountered tulips. He was the first Westerner to mention their existence in known writings from that period.

Religious intolerance forced Clusius to leave Vienna in 1593 to go to the Netherlands, a country more tolerant of his Protestant beliefs. He took tulips in the collection he brought with him, and planted them in Leiden's botanical garden, the first in Western Europe.

Clusius was very stingy with his bulbs, refusing to give any away or even sell them, and a group of frustrated buyers stole part of Clusius' collection. Dutch commercial cultivation started slowly in

Tulip Patch

the early 1600s. The beautiful flower was rare, and the wealthy clamored to buy them.

The tulip became a status symbol. A buying frenzy ensued, the price escalated, and Tulipomania was underway. Between 1623 and 1637, the price of the "Semper Augustus" bulb variety rose 2,400%! At the height of the frenzy, three Semper Augustus bulbs cost three times as much as a house along one of Amsterdam's canals. In 1637, the market collapsed and many lost their fortunes.

The origin of the word "tulip" is unknown. One explanation for how the tulip got its name is its resemblance to the turban worn by many men in the Middle East and Central Asia, the name of which became "tulipa" in Latin. (Source: www.bulb.com; "A Rambling Romp through Tulip History.")

Materials

- Dupioni or Thai silk:
  - Dark orange, 1 yd
  - Yellow, 1 yd
  - Dark red, 1 yd
  - Cream, 1 yd
- Zippers, 16":
- Dark orange
- Yellow
- Dark red
- Matching threads:
  - Dark orange
  - Yellow
  - Dark red
  - Lime green
- Tear Away™, 1 yd
- Scissors
- Marking pencil

- Tape measure
- Ruler
- ³⁄₈" piping cord, 5 yd
- Sewing pins
- Sewing machine with satin stitch feature
- Three pillow forms: 16", 14", 12"
- Stencil making supplies (see page 9)
- Fabric paints:
  - Dark red
  - Orange
  - Yellow
  - Gold
  - Dark green
- Sponges
- Vinyl gloves
- Plastic sheeting

Tulip Patch

Instructions

Sewing skills are required for this project (inserting zippers, making bias tape, covering piping, and stitching piping to pillow fronts).

1 **Out of dark orange silk cut:**
One 17" x 17" front piece
Two 9" x 17" pieces

Out of yellow silk cut:
One 15" x 15" front piece
Two 8" x 15" piece
Sufficient 2"-wide bias strips to make 5$\frac{1}{2}$ ft of covered piping

Out of dark red silk cut:
One 13" x 13" front piece
Two 7" x 13" pieces
Sufficient 2"-wide bias strips to make 5 ft of covered piping

Out of cream silk, cut:
Three 7$\frac{1}{2}$" x 9" piece
Sufficient 2"-wide bias strips to make 4$\frac{1}{2}$ ft of covered piping

2 Mark a border 1$\frac{1}{4}$" from the edges of the cream pieces.

3 Cut tulip stencil (see page 9 for stencil making instructions).

4 Working on a surface covered with plastic sheeting, stencil tulips inside the border you marked on the cream silk pieces in Step 2. Combine colors to make bunches of red, yellow, and orange tulips. Blend gold paint into the green paint to make various shades of green for stenciling the tulip stalks. Allow to dry. Set paint following manufacturer's instructions if necessary.

5 Center the stenciled panel on each front piece. Pin in place.

6 Satin stitch the stenciled panel to pillow front along the 1$\frac{1}{4}$" border. Use red thread for the orange and yellow pillows and lime green thread for the red pillow.

7 Make bias tape. Cover cord piping with silk bias.

8 With right sides together, matching raw edges, stitch cord piping to pillow fronts using ½" seam. You will need to clip the piping to fit around pillow corners. Use cream cord piping on red pillow; red cord piping on yellow pillow; and yellow piping on orange pillow.

9 To join the piping ends smoothly, cut away some of the cord so that the ends meet snugly. Cut bias fabric on each end so it extends 1" beyond cord. Turn under bias edge by ½". Arrange ends so that the folded edges neatly finish piping. Pin ends in place.

10 Baste in place, stitching as close to the piping as you can. Use a zipper foot if you do not have a piping foot.

11 Insert zippers in pillow backs along 17" edge using ½" seam. Ensure that there is a 1" seam above and below the start and end of the zipper. Final size of pillow back will be the same as pillow front.

12 Open zipper. With right sides together join pillow front to pillow back using ½" seam. (Note: Don't forget to open zipper, otherwise you won't be able to turn pillow to right side.)

13 Zigzag or serge to finish inside seams. Turn pillow to right side. Pull a ³⁄₈" fringe around the edge of the stenciled panel. Insert pillow forms.

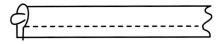

Encase cord piping
in silk bias.

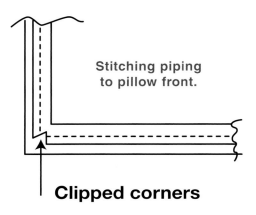

Stitching piping
to pillow front.

Clipped corners

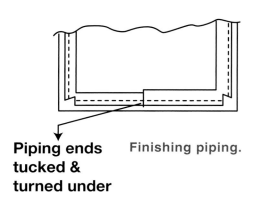

**Piping ends
tucked &
turned under**

Finishing piping.

Kuba-cloth Footstool

kuba cloth footstool.

*T*ransform a plain stool into a striking piece using a little wood varnish and Kuba cloth.

Design Tip

Upholster your footstool with Turkish kilim tapestries instead. There are so many wonderful patterns and colors to choose from, you are sure to find something to suit your taste.

Materials

- ☐ Unfinished wooden bench
- ☐ Kuba cloth (at least twice the surface of bench)
- ☐ Decorative trim (1½" x total length around bench. Choose color to match varnish or Kuba cloth)
- ☐ Upholstery foam, 2" thick (cut to fit top of bench)
- ☐ Wood varnish or stain
- ☐ Staple gun
- ☐ Gloves
- ☐ Glue
- ☐ Paper towels or sponges
- ☐ Scissors
- ☐ Old newspaper

Instructions

This project is suitable for all skill levels.

1 Cover work surface with old newspaper.

2 Using paper towels, varnish wooden stool. Apply second coat if necessary. Allow to dry between coats.

3 Glue upholstery foam to top of bench.

4 Measure Kuba cloth to size so that it covers top and sides of bench. To this size, add at least 3" to 4" so that Kuba cloth folds over underside of bench so there is sufficient to staple. Once you are comfortable with final measurements, cut piece of Kuba cloth to cover the bench.

5 Starting at one side, staple Kuba cloth to underside of bench. Work your way around the other three sides. Pull the cloth so that it fits well over the entire bench. Staple cloth on underside of bench.

6 Glue decorative trim over raw edge of Kuba cloth for a clean finish.

Rock Painting Wall Art

Rock painting wall stencil.

Rock painted wall art.

Rock paintings can be found in caves and rock surfaces all over the world. There are remarkably well-preserved famous rock paintings of Aboriginal rock art in Australia, of Bushman art in Southern Africa, of Native American Art in the Western United States, in Spain and Iceland, and in South America. These paintings give us a window into the culture, lives, and thoughts of our ancestors. In Australia, symbols of The Dreaming (Aboriginal stories of the Creation) are evident. In Spain, South Africa, and Iceland you can see depictions of hunting scenes and herds of wildlife. In the Western United States, images of corn maidens, wild life, warriors, animals, and everyday life are seen throughout Idaho, Utah, Colorado, Arizona, and New Mexico. Scholars have been successful at deciphering the messages in some of the stone art that remains around the world; however, much of it-particularly in cultures where no written record remains-is still a mystery to us. This simple project is inspired by famous rock engravings found at Twyfelfontein in Namibia (Southern Africa).

Rock Painting Wall Art

Materials

- ☐ Two strips balsa wood, $1/16$" x 4" x 36"
- ☐ Ochre colored wood stain
- ☐ Rust brown acrylic paint (I used Nova Color® 149 Transparent Red Iron Oxide)
- ☐ Clear wood varnish
- ☐ Sponges
- ☐ Paper plate
- ☐ Paintbrush with short, hard bristles
- ☐ Bowl of water
- ☐ White embossing powder
- ☐ Embossing heat tool
- ☐ Plastic surface covering
- ☐ Ruler
- ☐ Pencil
- ☐ Scissors
- ☐ Vinyl gloves
- ☐ Stencil making supplies (see page 9)
- ☐ Wall mounting adhesive squares (e.g. Scotch® Clear Mounting Squares)

Instructions

This project is suitable for all skill levels.

1 Cover work surface with plastic.

2 Measure and mark five 9" long sections on the balsa wood pieces. Make sure you mark lines across the width of the balsa wood.

3 Cut the balsa wood along each marked section.

4 Stain the front and sides of the balsa wood with ochre colored wood stain. Allow to dry.

5 Cut stencils of giraffe figures.

6 Using a paintbrush, place small amount of paint on paper plate. Rinse paintbrush.

7 Position sections of balsa wood alongside each other so the long edges are in contact. Using your cut stencils, and starting with a large giraffe, stencil first giraffe figures on section of balsa wood. Emboss figure immediately following stencil (follow manufacturer's instructions for using the embossing powder and heat tool).

8 Repeat stenciling and embossing process described in Step 6 above. You may have to position stencil so that it straddles edges of balsa wood. Alternate between large and small giraffe figures. Position animals in an order pleasing to you. Note: You must emboss each figure after it is stenciled, otherwise embossing will not work. Continue stenciling and embossing until all five balsa wood sections are covered.

9 Adhere sections of balsa wood to wall using adhesive squares. Leave approximately $1/8$" to $1/4$" space between each panel.

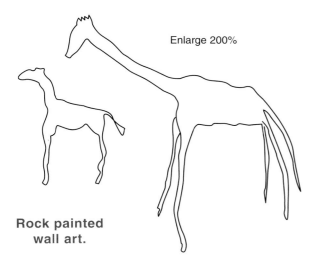

Enlarge 200%

Rock painted wall art.

Aztec Drinking Glass

Aztec glass.

Materials

- Drinking glass
- Contact® paper
- X-Acto knife or stencil burner
- Tracing paper
- Transfer paper
- Pencil
- Pen
- Scissors
- Masking tape
- Etching cream
- Craft lollipop stick
- Safety glasses
- Vinyl gloves
- Plastic sheeting

Lines and forms typical in Aztec art and artifacts inspired the pattern etched on this drinking glass. The pattern makes a strong, yet elegant, statement.

Design Tip

Etch this pattern on dinner plates or a pitcher to match the drinking glasses. Also consider decorating glass panes or a mirror with this pattern.

Aztec drinking glass pattern.

Instructions

This project is suitable for all skill levels (minors should be supervised and not permitted to apply etching cream). Read through all manufacturers' instructions for working with stencil burner and etching cream before starting. You may need additional supplies based on manufacturer's instructions. Wear safety glasses and gloves when working with etching cream.

1 Cover work surface with plastic sheeting.

2 Wash and dry drinking glass.

3 Copy Aztec pattern to tracing paper.

4 Cut a section of Contact paper at least ½" larger than the pattern. Using transfer paper, copy pattern to film side of Contact paper. You may have to tape Contact paper to work surface to prevent slipping.

5 Using X-Acto knife or stencil burner, cut out stencil of Aztec pattern.

6 Adhere stencil to the outside of the glass.

7 Following manufacturer's instructions, apply etching cream with lollipop stick. Do not apply etching cream beyond the edges of the Contact paper.

8 Allow to stand with etching cream for the length of time specified in manufacturer's instructions.

9 Rinse glass according to instructions.

Adinkra Coasters

Adinkra coasters.

T *hese great coasters will add sophisticated style to your drinks.*

Materials

- [ ] White card stock, 16" x 16"
- [ ] Strip balsa wood, 1/16" x 4" x 36"
- [ ] Acrylic paints:
    - Dark red
    - Gold
    - Bronze
- [ ] Sealer
- [ ] Wood varnish
- [ ] Paper plate
- [ ] Sponge brush
- [ ] Paintbrush with short, hard bristles
- [ ] Bowl of water
- [ ] Scissors
- [ ] Glue
- [ ] Plastic gloves
- [ ] Ruler
- [ ] Pencil
- [ ] Fine-tip black Sharpie® pen
- [ ] Stamp-making supplies (see page 16)

Adinkra Symbols

Adinkra symbols are among the most popular decorations used to convey an "ethnic" and "African" feel to craft and sewing projects today.

Adinkra is the name of a special cloth made and worn by the Akan people of Ghana and Côte d'Ivoire as part of funeral rites. Plain white or colored cloth is hand-painted and hand-embroidered with Adinkra symbols in a manner that conveys a specific parting message to the deceased. Adinkra literally translates into "a message one gives another when departing." The symbols express Akan worldview and reflect communal values, philosophy, social standards, and codes of conduct of the Akan people. They are visual symbols of proverbs, popular sayings, historical events, traits of behavior, and man-made and natural objects.

In popular American culture, they have transcended the solemn ritual that they are associated with in Africa, and are seen as appropriate symbols for everyday objects. Even in Ghana and Côte d'Ivoire, commercially printed Adinkra cloth is widely available, and is worn without the traditional formal associations. The symbols offer a great basic vocabulary for creating more complicated patterns. (Sources: *The Adinkra Dictionary*, Bruce Willis, The Pyramid Complex, Washington, D.C., 1998. *Adinkra Wall Poster*, Dr. Kwaku Ofori-Ansa, Sankofa Publications, Maryland).

Adinkra Coasters

Instructions

This project is suitable for all skill levels.
Between steps, rinse paintbrush and sponge brush as necessary.

1 Cut 1" x 1" Adinkra stamps in your desired patterns (see page 16).

2 Cut four 4" x 4" squares out of white cardstock.

3 Cut four 4" x 4" squares out of balsa wood.

4 Glue cardstock to balsa wood squares.

5 Brush a coat of sealer over card stock using sponge brush. Allow to dry.

6 Using paintbrush, place small amounts of each paint color on paper plate.

7 Working in light strokes using sponge brush, cover white cardstock with a base coat of bronze paint. Allow to dry. Tip: Vary the shades of bronze on each square.

8 Apply light layer of contrasting red and bronze acrylic paint to Adinkra stamp. Stamp Adinkra patterns over painted surface of cardstock in desired arrangement. (I used simple square patterns.) Blend shades of lighter bronze and red to create varying shades. Allow to dry. Rinse stamps.

9 Hand draw lines and squares around the stamped patterns with Sharpie® pen.

10 Brush two coats of varnish over finished coaster using sponge brush. Allow to dry between coats.

Adinkrahene. King of the Adinkra symbols. Symbol of greatness, prudence, firmness, and magnanimity.

Akoma. Means: "The heart." Symbol of love, goodwill, patience, faithfulness, fondness, endurance, and consistency.

Nsoroma. Means: "A child of the Heavens, Star." Symbol of faith and belief in the dependency on a supreme being.

Dwennimmen. Means: "Rams Horns." Symbol of strength, humility, wisdom, and learning.

Odo Nyera Fie Kwan. Means: "Love never loses its way home." Symbol of love and devotion.

Nyame Dua. Means: "An Altar of God." Symbol of God's presence and protection.

The Moon and the Star. Symbol of faithfulness, fondness, harmony, love, loyalty, and femininity.

Asase Ye Duro. Means: "The Earth is Heavy (mysterious, non-trivial)." Symbol of the providence and divinity of Mother Earth.

Fofo. Means: "Seeds of a plant."When the small yellow petals of the fofo plant drop, they turn into black spiky seeds. The Akan liken the nature of this plant to that of a jealous person. Symbol warning against jealousy and covetousness.

Gyawa Atiko. Means: "The back of Gyawu's head." A hairstyle worn by Gyawu-a royal attendant. Symbol of Gyawu's escape.

Gye Nyame. Means: "I am afraid of none, except God." Symbol of omnipotence, omnipresence, and supremacy of God.

Krapa. Means: "Thing for sacrifice." Symbol of spiritual balance, good fortune, good luck, sanctity, spiritual strength, and uprightness of spirit.

Tabono. Means: "Paddle, oar." Symbol of strength, confidence, and persistence.

Another depiction of Sankofa.

Sankofa. Means "Go back to the past to build for the future." Symbol of the wisdom of learning from the past.

Sunsum. Means: "The Soul." Symbol of spirituality, spiritual purity, and cleanliness of the soul.

Kente Wall Panel

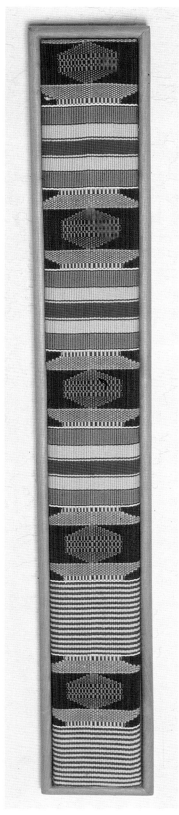

Kente wall panel.

A mounted wall panel is a simple yet interesting way to display your Kente cloth.

Design Tip

Don't have Kente? Don't like Kente? No problem. Use other woven or ethnic fabrics instead.

Materials

- ❏ Kente cloth, 6" x 34"
- ❏ ¼" thick foam, 4" x 30"
- ❏ Balsa wood, ¼" x 4" x 30"
- ❏ Spray adhesive
- ❏ Staple gun
- ❏ Scissors
- ❏ Vinyl gloves

Instructions

This project is suitable for all skill levels.

Professional services are needed to frame the wall panel, but if you are comfortable with framing, you may frame your panel yourself. Framing supplies are not included in the supply list.

1 Using spray adhesive, glue the foam to one side of balsa wood.

2 Center the Kente cloth over the foam. You will have about ½" excess fabric along either long edge and 2" excess along the short edges of the panel.

3 Working from the back of the panel, pull fabric over balsa wood and staple in place. Ensure that fabric is pulled taut and edges are smooth when you staple fabric.

4 Have panel framed by professional framer, or frame it yourself.

Mudcloth Mirror

Mudcloth mirror.

Mudcloth samples.

Simple strips of mudcloth transform a plain mirror into something special. It's a perfect no-sew project for incorporating your strip woven fabric into handsome additions for your home.

Mudcloth

Mudcloth was probably one of the most influential "ethnic" fabrics in the 1990s-a lofty claim to make for a handmade cotton fabric from Mali in West Africa. But so far-reaching has been this lowly cloth's influence, that today chic people adorn everything from pillows and clothing, to CDs and book covers with the colors and motifs of mudcloth.

Made by the Bamana people of Mali, the name mudcloth derives from the literal translation of the indigenous name "bogolanfini," which means "traces of mud." Making mudcloth is labor intensive. Women decorate plain, woven cotton fabric with geometric motifs in a repetitive process that uses vegetable dyes in a technique that researchers date back as far as the 1200s. Most mudcloth is dyed in earth tones; however, in response to market demand, artists now offer fabric in a wide range of bright colors including red, purple, green, and orange. (Source: *African Fabrics*, Ronke Luke-Boone, Krause Publications, 2001).

Mudcloth Mirror

Materials

- Mirror, 24" x 36"
- Balsa wood, four pieces ⅛" x 6" x 36"
- Dark brown mudcloth, 1½ yd long
- Leather scraps
- Leather glue
- Glue gun
- Ruler
- Pen
- Scissors
- Craft knife
- Glass cleaner
- Paper towels
- Binder clips

Instructions

This project is suitable for all skill levels.
Professional framing services are needed. Minors should be supervised. Adjust measurements to fit mirror of different size.

1 Clean mirror with glass cleaner and paper towels.

2 Out of balsa wood, cut two 3" x 36" strips and two 3" x 24" strips. Miter the edges of balsa wood to dimensions shown in illustration.

3 Out of mudcloth, cut two 4" x 39" pieces and two 4" x 26" pieces. Miter the edges of the mudcloth to dimensions shown in illustration.

4 Lay mudcloth on work surface right side down, so wrong side faces you. Center balsa wood strips on fabric. Using glue gun, apply beads of glue along edge of fabric and fold over and glue onto balsa wood. You may have to hold in place briefly with binder clip until fabric adheres. Ensure that angled corners are covered smoothly.

5 Turn strips to right side. Cut strips of leather large enough to cover joint between pieces. Using leather glue, glue leather onto mudcloth to cover joint at the mitered corners. You will form a large rectangle border with an open space for the mirror. Allow to dry.

6 Unless you frame it yourself, take the mirror and rectangular mudcloth border to a professional framing service for final assembly and framing.

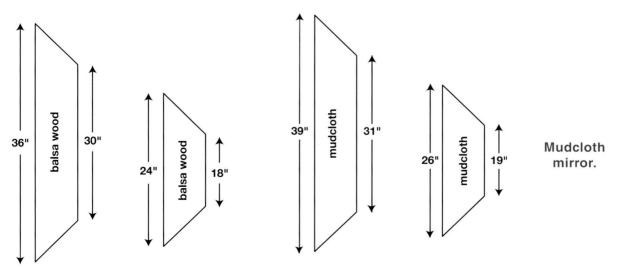

Mudcloth mirror.

Australian Aboriginal Flower Pot

Dot paintings are a well-recognized genre of Australian Aboriginal art that is sought after and prized by art collectors. The artist creates forms or fills areas with dots of varying size and color. The contrast in size and colors of the dots results in very striking images. This simple pot is inspired by this ancient art form. Research Australian Aboriginal art to see how complex and inspiring dot paintings can be.

Materials

- ❏ Unfinished clay pot
- ❏ Clay or terra cotta paints
- ❏ Sponges
- ❏ Stencil spray adhesive
- ❏ Spray sealer
- ❏ Fine tipped paintbrush
- ❏ Vinyl gloves
- ❏ Plastic sheeting
- ❏ Stencil making supplies (see page 9)

Instructions

This project is suitable for all skill levels.

1 Cut stencils of Aboriginal watering hole motif (or motif of your choice). See page 9 for guidance.

2 Cover work surface with plastic sheeting.

3 Adhere stencil to clay pot using spray adhesive.

4 Stencil watering hole pattern to pot using sponges. Remove stencil and allow to dry. Stencil several motifs over pot surface.

5 Paint dots in contrasting paint to fill areas between rings. Allow to dry.

6 Spray sealant over pot surface. Allow to dry.

Flowerpot stencil.

Mountain Sheep Plant Pot

Mountain sheep flower pot.

M y inspiration for this project was a book on rock paintings in the western United States that included the Great Hunting Scene found in Nine Mile Canyon in northeastern Utah. The mountain sheep clay pot is a simple, yet perfect, container for cactus and other western plants.

The Great Hunting Scene

The Great Hunting Scene found in Nine Mile Canyon in northeastern Utah is one of the best examples of native rock art in the Western United States. Several human figures, some bearing shields, others believed to be camouflaged in hides, are seen shooting arrows at a flock of over 30 bighorn sheep. The entire composition is hand-chiseled into the rock. While the scene obviously depicts a hunting event, there are still details within the composition that researchers have not been able to decipher.

Instructions

This project is suitable for all skill levels. Eliminate stencil spray adhesive if you cut stencils out of Contact paper.

1 Cut stencils of mountain sheep.

2 Cover work surface with plastic sheeting.

3 Lightly spray paint clay pot white. The covering should be uneven and the terracotta pot surface should be visible. Allow to dry.

4 Adhere mountain goats to the clay pot using spray adhesive. Place larger goats on bottom and small goats around rim. Allow to dry between stenciling as necessary.

5 Spray sealant over pot surface. Allow to dry.

Materials

- ☐ Unfinished clay pot
- ☐ White spray paint
- ☐ Rust brown acrylic paints (I used Nova Color® 149 Transparent Red Iron Oxide)
- ☐ Sponges
- ☐ Stencil spray adhesive
- ☐ Spray sealer
- ☐ Vinyl gloves
- ☐ Plastic sheeting
- ☐ Stencil making supplies (see page 9)

Mountain sheep.

Hopi Gold Leaf Cactus Planter

Gold leaf Hopi-pattern cactus planter.

G *old leaf and Hopi patterns add flair to a simple container.*

Materials

- ☐ Clear glass container, 8" x 2½" x 2½"
- ☐ Gold leaf kit
- ☐ Red glass paint pen
- ☐ Tracing paper
- ☐ Pen
- ☐ Scotch® tape
- ☐ Vinyl gloves
- ☐ Safety glasses
- ☐ Plastic sheeting

Instructions

This project is suitable for all skill levels (minors should be supervised when working with gold leaf). Review manufacturer's instructions for using glass paint and gold leaf before starting. You may require additional supplies based on manufacturer's instructions. Optional: You may eliminate the gold leaf and just paint pattern onto glass planter.

1 Cover work surface with plastic sheeting.

2 Copy Hopi pattern onto tracing paper.

3 Tape tracing paper on the inside of glass container.

4 On outside of glass, trace pattern using paint pen. Allow to dry. Cure paint according to manufacturer's instructions.

5 Following manufacturer's instructions, apply gold leaf to inside of glass container.

6 Adhere gold leaf to inside of glass. Brush away excess gold leaf.

7 Apply gold leaf sealer and allow to dry according to manufacturer's instructions.

Mehndi–Henna Bed Linen

Add an exotic flair to your bed linen by stenciling this Mehndi/henna-inspired border across the edge of the top sheet and pillowcases. The pattern on your bed linen will last longer than traditional henna body painting.

Design Tip

Decorate throw pillows with henna border or all-over patterns.

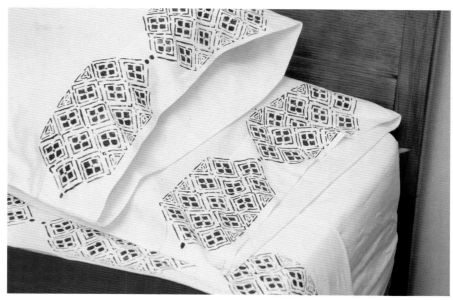

Henna bed linen.

Moroccan Berber Henna Motifs

For thousands of years, women in Africa, India, and the Middle East have transformed their hands and feet-if only for a short time-into intricate works of red-hued art with henna. Patterns can be so intricate and exquisite that hands and feet can appear like bejeweled gloves and slippers.

Henna is believed to have protective and healing powers, bring good luck, beautify, and provide for spiritual protection and material well-being. As such, henna body painting (referred to as Mehndi in India) is an integral part of celebrating rites of passage such as weddings, births, child-naming ceremonies, and burials. Customs and henna uses vary across the world. For brides throughout the Middle East, Africa, and India, henna decoration is an important part of wedding rituals. In the north and western parts of India, custom says the deeper the henna color obtained on the skin, the longer the love will last between the couple. In their seventh month of pregnancy, Moroccan women have specific symbols, which will protect mother and child during birth, painted on their ankles. Regardless of where, skilled henna practitioners play important roles in their societies.

Patterns also vary. In Africa, patterns tend to be more

Mauritanian woman with henna-decorated hands.

geometric. The motifs (page 46) from Morocco's Berbers are an example of how natural objects are translated into geometric shapes.

In the Middle East, large floral patterns are more common. In India, henna patterns tend to be intricate, lacy, floral, and paisley patterns.

The henna plant originated in Egypt. From there, it spread to other parts of Africa, the Middle East and India. The tiny leaves of the henna shrub are dried and made into a powder that is used to make the paste used for body painting.

Henna painting exploded into American popular culture in the mid 1990s. Celebrities, youth, and regular folk have adorned their bodies with henna designs and patterns. Unlike tattooing, which is painful and permanent, henna appeals to every one because there is no pain and so much to gain with these beautiful body paintings. Skilled henna practitioners can be found in every major city in the United States today, and henna kits are available through Web sites and even major craft retailers. (Sources: "Henna and the Moroccan Aesthetic," Lisa Butterworth, http://www.kenzi.com, *Mehndi*, Carine Fabius, Three Rivers Press, New York, 1998.)

Mehndi–Henna Bed Linen

Materials

- ☐ Bed linen
- ☐ Deep red fabric paint
- ☐ Stencil brush
- ☐ Stencil making supplies (see page 9)
- ☐ Plastic sheeting
- ☐ Vinyl gloves
- ☐ Stencil spray adhesive
- ☐ Iron
- ☐ Masking tape
- ☐ Weights (or soup cans)

Moraccan Berber Henna Symbols

Spider
Associated with fertility and magical rites.

Lion's Paw
Symbol of strength; the claws are a symbol of protection.

Finger
A protective symbol.

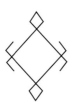

Frog
Associated with fertility and magical rites.

Partridge Eyes
Symbol of women and beauty.

Sources: Lisa Butterworth Maison Kenzi; www.kenzi.com

Eye
Symbol of protection against the Evil Eye. The cross in the center deflects evil in four directions.

Instructions

This project is suitable for all skill levels.

1 Make stencil following directions on page 9.

2 Press pillowcases and top sheet. Fold and mark mid-point of short edge of pillowcases and top edge of sheet.

3 Cover work surface with plastic sheeting.

4 Place top sheet over protected work surface. Use weights to prevent sheet from slipping off table, or tape sheet to work surface.

Enlarge stencil by 133%

5 Starting at the midpoint, stencil Mehndi pattern across top edge of sheet. Use stencil spray to hold stencil in place. Work progressively from center toward outer edge of sheet until entire length is complete. Allow to dry between stencils as necessary. Follow manufacturer's instructions for setting the paint.

6 Cut piece of plastic sheeting to fit snugly across the length of the pillow case opening. Place plastic sheeting inside the pillowcase inside opening. This will prevent ink from bleeding through to other side of pillowcase.

7 Starting at midpoint of pillowcase edge, stencil the Mehndi pattern across the opening of the pillowcase as described in Step 4. Allow to dry. Follow manufacturer's instructions for setting the paint.

Feather Silk Pillows

Turn a simple silk pillow into a stunning, exotic accent with peacock, and other brightly colored feathers.

Feathers and the Aztec

The Aztecs used brightly colored feathers from tropical birds to adorn their headdresses, shields, fans, and other everyday and special occasion artifacts. Elaborate decorations, including animal and bird designs, were added to shields by gluing feathers onto surfaces. Sometimes the patterns were outlined in gold. To the Aztec, the green feathers from the quetzal bird, linked to the Aztec god Quetzalcoatl, were the most precious of all. One of the most spectacular examples of Aztec headdresses is the one Moctezuma II sent with Cortes as a gift to the King of Spain. The headdress was made of the things the Aztecs treasured most- gold, precious stones, turquoise, and green feathers from tropical birds.

Feather silk pillow.

Materials

- ❑ Purple silk pillow
- ❑ Peacock feather
- ❑ Blue feather
- ❑ Green feather
- ❑ ½" wide purple ribbon, 1 yd
- ❑ Matching purple thread
- ❑ Decorative gold button (optional)
- ❑ Rubber band
- ❑ Sewing pins
- ❑ Needle
- ❑ Purchased pillows

Instructions

This project is suitable for all skill levels.

1 Arrange the peacock feathers below the blue and green feathers in an arrangement pleasing to you. Secure positions with rubber band.

2 Conceal the rubber band and secure the feathers by wrapping them together with the ribbon. Secure ribbon with small stitches.

3 (Optional) Position gold button over the ribbon and stitch in place.

4 Position the feather arrangement on the pillow. Pin in place. Hand stitch the arrangement to the pillow.

Linen and Brocade Throw

A *throw casually draped over a sofa or chaise is a great way to add a decorative element to a living space. This elegant throw features a brocade center panel bordered on each end with panels consisting of alternating linen, Korhogo cloth, and mudcloth blocks. Mudcloth and Korhogo cloth add an exotic twist to a timeless piece.*

Linen and brocade throw.

Korhogo Cloth

Korhogo cloth is a cotton fabric, handmade from handspun cotton by the Senufo people. It is named after the town of Korhogo in Côte d'Ivoire (West Africa). It is often mistaken for a variation of mudcloth. With the exceptions of the similarities in weaving the basic cotton cloth, there is no similarity in the techniques for decorating these fabrics. Korhogo cloth is easily recognizable by the distinct animal and human figures that decorate the cloth.

Each figure has a distinct meaning: fish depict life and water; fish bones depict drought, and lions depict royal power. Within Senufo society, Korhogo cloth is commissioned and worn for specific purposes-hunters wear cloth for protection and camouflage when hunting. However, most of the cloth made for export does not have any of the significance attributed to traditional uses. In the U.S. and Europe, Korhogo cloth is often used for making pillows, wall hangings, and other home decorations. (Source: *African Fabrics*, Ronke Luke-Boone, Krause, WI, 2001.)

Sample of Korhogo cloth.

Linen and Brocade Throw

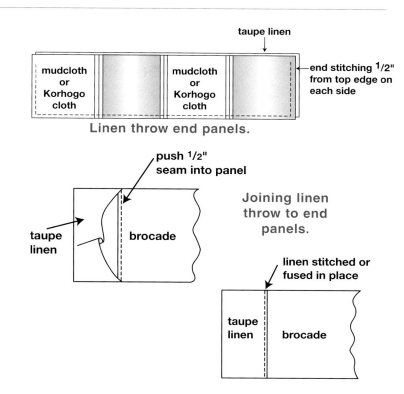

Materials

- ❏ 60"-wide off-white brocade, 2 yds
- ❏ 60"-wide taupe linen, 1 yd
- ❏ Korhogo cloth, 1 yd
- ❏ Mudcloth, 1 yd
- ❏ Fusible web (e.g. Stitch witchery®)
- ❏ Matching thread
- ❏ Cowerie shells or beads (optional)
- ❏ Scissors
- ❏ Tape measure

taupe linen

mudcloth or Korhogo cloth | mudcloth or Korhogo cloth

← end stitching 1/2" from top edge on each side

Linen throw end panels.

push 1/2" seam into panel

taupe linen — brocade

Joining linen throw to end panels.

linen stitched or fused in place

taupe linen ┆ brocade

Instructions

Machine sewing skills are required for this project.
Wash Korhogo cloth and mudcloth prior to starting. For additional guidance for working with Korhogo cloth and mudcloth, see *African Fabrics* by Ronke Luke-Boone, Krause Publications, 2001.

1 **Out of taupe linen, cut:**
Two 16" x 16" pieces
Two 16" x 60" pieces

Out of Korhogo cloth, cut:
Two 16" x 16" pieces

Out of mudcloth cut:
Two 16" x 16" pieces

2 Turn under a ½" seam along both selvedges of the brocade. Press. Stitch in place.

3 With right sides together, stitch mudcloth, Korhogo, and linen panels together using a ½" seam. Alternate linen panels with the mudcloth and Korhogo cloth panels. Trim seams and press open.

4 Along one 60" edge of the remaining taupe panel, turn under and press a ½" seam to the wrong side.

5 With right sides together, raw edges matching, join the taupe linen piece to the panel piece using a ½" seam. End stitching ½" from raw edge at seam turned under in Step 4. Trim seam. Clip corners if necessary.

6 With right sides together, raw edges even, stitch a joined panel to each end of the brocade center using a ½" seam. Be careful not to catch the turned under seam on the taupe piece. Press.

7 Tuck the seam into the panels. Fuse in place with fusible web. Note: You may stitch in place instead of fusing.

8 (Optional) Hand stitch cowerie shells or beads over the throw randomly as you wish.

Paper-covered Lampshade

Decorative paper lampshade.

Can't find the exact color and texture lampshade to suit your decor? Make your own. Handmade craft papers are available in an amazing array of colors and textures. They are an easy way to create the lampshade perfect for your space. This paper-covered lampshade is an easy project to get you started.

Materials

- ❐ Sheets of decorative paper (matching or contrasting)
- ❐ Self-adhesive lampshade
- ❐ Tracing paper
- ❐ Pen
- ❐ Scissors
- ❐ Beaded trim (sufficient to go around lampshade bottom)
- ❐ Glue gun

Instructions

This project is suitable for all skill levels.
Before starting, review manufacturer's instructions for using self-adhesive lampshade.

1 Remove pattern form from lampshade.

2 Trace outline of shade pattern on to tracing paper.

3 Draw design of your choice onto traced pattern. Design ideas: horizontal and vertical stripes or collage.

4 Trace patterns of the design sections from Step 3 onto tracing paper. Cut out these sections.

5 Cut design sections out of decorative papers.

6 Adhere paper sections to lampshade following your design in Step 3.

7 Use glue gun to adhere beaded trip to bottom rim of lampshade.

Wall Hanging Rod & Sand-dipped Finials

ang your Aboriginal or African safari wall panels on your own special rod. Here's an easy one that will go perfectly with either wall panel.

Materials

- ☐ Wood dowel, 36" x 1/2" diameter
- ☐ Wood varnish or stain
- ☐ Small Styrofoam® balls
- ☐ General purpose glue
- ☐ Sponge brush
- ☐ Gloves
- ☐ Colored art sand
- ☐ Paper plate
- ☐ Paper towels or sponges

Instructions

This project is suitable for all skill levels.

1 Push dowel into Styrofoam ball to make a cavity in ball. Be careful not to push dowel through Styrofoam ball. The dowel will rest in this cavity.

2 Using paper towels, apply two coats of varnish to dowel. Allow to dry.

3 Pour a small pile of each color of sand onto paper plate.

4 Using the sponge brush, apply glue to section of Styrofoam ball. Dip ball into colored sand, covering surface. Repeat process of applying glue to ball and dipping into sand until the surface completely covered. You may need to allow it to dry between dippings.

5 Once dry, glue sand-covered ball to end of dowel, by squeezing glue into the cavity you created in Step 1.

3 | Cool Blues
with a Hint of Red

Here is a group of wonderful projects that set a sophisticated
tone with cool blues, silver, and a hint of red.

Adire Director's Chair

Adire director's chair.

White and light patterns against deep indigo fabrics makes Adire an attractive fabric and inspired this striking director's chair. Typical Adire motifs are stenciled against a deep blue canvas creating an attractive chair. This is a very simple project with very dramatic results.

Design Tip

You can use the same pattern to decorate other chairs or surfaces in your home. Simply paint the surface blue and stencil over with Adire patterns in pale blue or pearl blue.

Adire Eleko-Fabric Art from Nigeria

Adire Eleko is an indigo-dyed cloth made by Yoruba women of Southwest Nigeria since about 1910. "Adire" is a Yoruba word that means "to take to tie and to dye." Today the word Adire is used as a general term to refer to a resist-dyed cloth. Eleko is one of the resist techniques used to make Adire by which the pattern is hand-drawn or stenciled on the cloth using a paste (or eko).

Making Adire is women's work, and women apprentice for many years to learn the skills required to produce the beautiful textile. Starting with white cotton shirting, the artist draws patterns onto the cloth using a paste, which is made from cassava flour (lafum), alum, and copper sulfate. The alum bonds the paste to the fibers of the cloth, and the copper sulfate acts as a preservative. Intricate patterns are drawn over the entire fabric surface by one of two means: free-hand, using the tip of a knife,

feather, or spine of palm, or using a metal stencil. When the pattern is completed, the cloth is hung in the sun to dry until the eko is hard.

The dry cloth is next dyed blue by a skilled dyer (alaro) in a dye bath made using the leaves of the indigo plant (elu). Indigo dyeing is a lengthy process as the cloth must dipped many times into the dye bath to reach the desired depth of color. The dyed cloth is hung to dry. Once dry, the paste (eko) is scraped off to reveal pale blue designs on an indigo background.

Adire is sold in markets in Nigeria, or can be purchased or commissioned directly from a skilled artist known as an alAdire. (Source: *Alaro*, An Activity Pack for 7-11 year olds based on textiles from South-West Nigeria, Smithsonian Institution, Museum of African Art, 1989).

Materials

- ❏ Dark blue director's chair seat covering
- ❏ Pearl blue fabric paint (I used Nova Color's® #165 Blue Pearl)
- ❏ Plastic dish or paper plate
- ❏ Stencil brush and sponges
- ❏ Stencil spray adhesive
- ❏ Weights (or soup cans)
- ❏ Masking tape (optional)
- ❏ Pencil
- ❏ Ruler or tape measure
- ❏ Stencil making supplies (see page 9)
- ❏ Plastic sheeting
- ❏ Vinyl gloves

Instructions

This project is suitable for all skill levels.
You may require additional supplies based on paint manufacturer's instructions.

1 Make Adire stencil following guidelines on page 9.

2 Cover work surface with plastic sheeting.

3 Using tape measure and pencil, mark center of chair seat and back.

4 Place chair seat on sheeting. Place weights at the corners to hold in place (you may also use masking tape).

5 Place small amount of paint on your paint dish. Starting at the center and working toward the sides, stencil alternating Adire patterns on the seat and back. You may have to allow sections to dry before continuing to avoid getting paint on the bottom of your stencil.

6 Follow manufacturer's instructions for setting the paint.

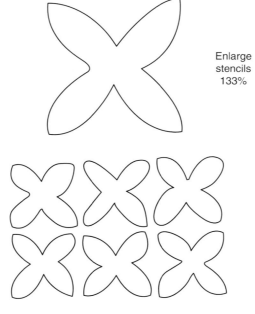

Grid line stencil. Lengthen and shorten as necessary

Enlarge stencils 133%

Adire director's chair stencils

Hopi-Patterned Plate

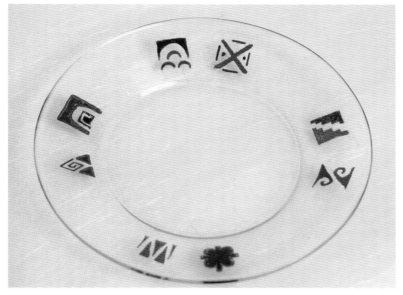

Hopi-patterned plate.

H opi patterns transform a plain glass plate into an attractive piece. The geometric patterns add an attractive abstract element to the plates. Decorate a set of plates in matching patterns or use multiple patterns on each plate. Either way, you'll create great place settings with these Hopi-inspired plates.

The Hopi

Hopi means "people of peace." The Hopi live in 12 villages situated atop or at the foot of the First, Second, and Third Mesas in northeast Arizona. ("Mesa" comes from the Spanish word for table. A mesa is a broad, flat-topped elevation with one or more cliff-like sides.) The villages are independent of each other and are self-governed by traditional leadership or an elected board of directors. Each village holds its ceremonies in accordance to village leadership. For defensive purposes, the Hopis camouflaged their dwellings, making them difficult to detect atop mesas. While the defensive need no longer exists today, dwellings may still be camouflaged. The Hopi have the distinction of being the only group of Native Americans to have continuously inhabited the same area dating back to A.D. 500. Unfortunately, they have lost about 90 percent of their original land. Today the Hopi reservation is completely surrounded by the Navajo.

Hopi are very spiritual. Kachinas play an important role in Hopi religion and culture. They are spiritual entities that can represent the spirit of the ancestors, deities of the natural world, or intermediaries between man and God. Kachinas intercede on behalf of the Hopi, bringing rain, curing disease, and meting out punishment.

The Hopi are the most traditional of all the North American native tribes, and take great pride in living the old way. Because of their great reverence for their traditions, the Hopi have been able to preserve much more of their artistic traditions and produce high quality art. Hopi paintings, baskets, pottery, and jewelry are highly sought after, and the finer works can command high prices. (Sources: Kuwawata, Welcome to the Official Site of the Hopi Tribe, http://www.hopi.nsn.us/, About the Hopi Indians, http://www.3mesas.com/hopi/main.html, Hopi Indians, http://inkido.indiana.edu/w310work/romac/hopi.htm.)

Materials

- ❐ Plain, clear glass plate
- ❐ Contact® paper
- ❐ Blue glass paint pen
- ❐ Red glass paint pen
- ❐ Tracing paper
- ❐ Pen
- ❐ Pencil
- ❐ Transfer paper (carbon paper)
- ❐ Scissors

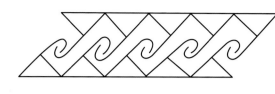

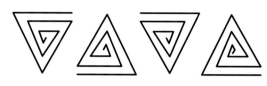

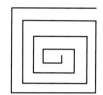

Instructions

This project is suitable for all skill levels.
Carefully review manufacturer's instructions for using glass paint pens. You may require additional supplies based on manufacturer's instructions.

1 Wash and dry plate.

2 Copy Hopi patterns onto tracing paper.

3 Using transfer paper, copy Hopi patterns onto Contact paper. Allow at least ¾" of Contact paper around each pattern.

4 Cut out Hopi patterns, allowing ½" of Contact paper around each pattern.

5 Peel and stick patterns on the right side of plate rim. (This is particularly important if manufacturer's guidelines state that paint is unsuitable for food contact.) Arrange patterns in manner pleasing to you around the rim.

6 Working on the underside (back) of plate, using blue and red paint paints, outline Hopi patterns. Fill in some patterns, as you desire.

7 Allow to dry and follow manufacturers instructions to set paint.

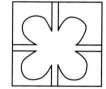
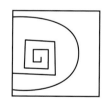
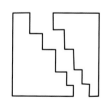
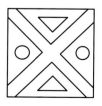
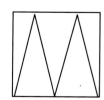

Painting Hopi plate.

Moroccan-tile Inspired Plate

Moroccan tile plate.

Moroccan tile patterns add an exotic touch to a jewel-tone plate. This simple project transforms plates into elegant pieces.

Instructions

This project is suitable for all skill levels.
Carefully review manufacturer's instructions for using glass paint pens. You may require additional supplies based on manufacturer's instructions.

1 Wash and dry plate or clean with glass cleaner.

2 Copy tile pattern onto tracing paper.

3 Using transfer paper, copy tile patterns onto Contact paper. Allow at least ¾" of Contact paper around pattern.

4 Cut out tile pattern, allowing ½" of Contact paper around each pattern.

5 Peel and stick patterns on right side of plate rim. (This is particularly important if manufacturer's guidelines state that paint is unsuitable for food contact.)

6 Working on the underside (back) of plate, outline Moroccan-tile pattern.

7 Repeat Steps 4 and 5 until you decorate the rim in a manner pleasing to you.

8 Allow to dry. Follow manufacturers instructions to set paint.

Materials

- ☐ Transparent blue glass plate
- ☐ Contact® paper
- ☐ Blue glass paint pen
- ☐ Tracing paper
- ☐ Pen
- ☐ Pencil
- ☐ Transfer paper (carbon paper)
- ☐ Scissors
- ☐ Glass cleaner (optional)

Painting Moroccan tile plate.

Blue Aztec Drinking Glass

Blue Aztec drinking glass.

T he Aztecs loved music, singing, dancing, and poetry. The floral pattern on this Mexican handblown glass is one of several that decorate the Aztec statue of Xochipilli, "the flower prince." This project is a great way to add Mexican history to a present-day popular article—handblown drinking glasses.

Materials

- ❑ Mexican handblown drinking glass (usually have hints of blue and/or green in the glass)
- ❑ Blue glass paint pen
- ❑ Tracing paper
- ❑ Pencil
- ❑ Scissors
- ❑ Scotch® tape

Instructions

This project is suitable for all skill levels.
Read manufacturer's instructions for using glass paint. You may need additional supplies based on manufacturer's instructions.

1 Wash and dry glass.

2 Copy Aztec floral pattern to tracing paper. Cut out pattern.

3 Tape pattern to inside of glass.

4 Using paint pen, copy the outline of the floral pattern on outside of glass. If you are using a paint that prohibits contact with food, ensure that the pattern is placed below the drinking rim. Allow to dry.

5 Repeat Steps 3 and 4 until you have sufficient patterns (to your liking) on the glass. Allow to dry between applications if necessary.

6 Following manufacturer's instructions for curing the paint if necessary.

Aztec drinking glass pattern.

Adire Coasters

Adire coasters.

A nother set of simple-to-make coasters that add sophisticated style to your drink enjoyment.

Instructions

This project is suitable for all skill levels.

1 Follow instructions for making Adinkra Coasters (see page 37), replacing Adinkra stamps with Adire stamps.

2 Using paintbrush, prepare a small amount of light blue paint on the paper plate by blending the ultramarine blue and silver paint. Rinse paintbrush as necessary.

3 Working in light strokes with the sponge brush, paint the white cardstock light blue. You may vary the shades of light blue on each square. Allow to dry. Rinse sponge brush.

Materials

- ☐ Sheet white card stock
- ☐ Strip balsa wood, ¹⁄₁₆" x 4"x 36"
- ☐ Ultramarine blue acrylic paint
- ☐ Silver acrylic paint (I used Nova Color® 122 Ultramarine Blue and Nova Color® 137 Silver)
- ☐ Sealer
- ☐ Wood varnish
- ☐ Paper plate
- ☐ Sponge brush
- ☐ Paintbrush with short, hard bristles
- ☐ Bowl of water
- ☐ Scissors
- ☐ Glue
- ☐ Vinyl gloves
- ☐ Ruler
- ☐ Pencil
- ☐ Stamp-making supplies (see page 14)

Silver Leaf Votive

Silver leaf votive.

*T*he disco era, with its fabulous spinning disco lights, inspired this votive! Silver leaf and glass paint transform a simple votive into something shiny and special.

Design Tip
Try gold leaf for a regal finish.

Materials

☐ Clear glass votive
☐ Silver leaf kit
☐ Frosted glass paint pens:
   Blue
   Green
   Red
☐ Vinyl gloves
☐ Plastic sheeting

Instructions

This project is suitable for all skill levels
(minors should be supervised when working with silver leaf). Review manufacturer's instructions for using glass paint and silver leaf before starting. You may require additional supplies based on manufacturer's instructions.

1 Wash and dry glass votive.

2 Cover work surface with plastic sheeting.

3 Using paint pens, make small, random-colored dots on the outer surface of the votive. Allow to dry.

4 Cure paint according to manufacturer's instructions.

5 Follow manufacturer's instructions and apply silver leaf to the inside of the votive.

Beaded Napkin Rings

Beaded napkin rings.

Add sparkle to your table setting with these beaded napkin rings, inspired by India's famous beaded textiles. The rich, vibrant colors, intricate details, and fine craftsmanship combine to make spectacular textiles that are desired world wide. They are so easy to make, you could make many different colors to match your changing décor.

Design Tip

Put your own spin on it! Mix two or more bead colors together, or apply beads in bands of alternating or varying colors.

Materials

- ❑ Packet of small seed beads (blue or desired color)
- ❑ All purpose glue
- ❑ Sponge brush
- ❑ Acrylic paint in color to match beads
- ❑ Paintbrush
- ❑ Plain wooden napkin rings
- ❑ Paper plate
- ❑ Vinyl gloves
- ❑ Plastic sheeting or old newspaper

Instructions

This project is suitable for all skill levels.

1 Cover work surface with plastic sheeting or newspaper.

2 Paint inside and outside surfaces of napkin rings. Allow to dry.

3 Sprinkle seed beads onto paper plate in a small pile.

4 Using sponge brush, apply glue onto outside of napkin ring. Dip ring into pile of beads until area is completely covered. Repeat process around the napkin ring until entire surface is covered with beads. Allow to dry between dipping as necessary.

Henna/Mehndi Inspired Napkins

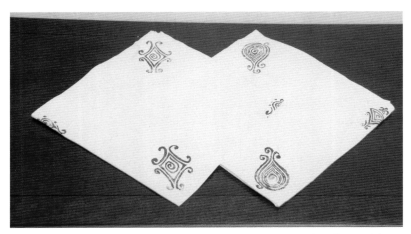

Mehndi napkins.

Curls and swirls of henna and Mehndi patterns add pretty touches to simple white napkins-and an elegant touch to your table setting.

Design Tip

Put your own spin on these pretty napkins by using colored napkins; using different colored paint; varying the positions of the stamped patterns on each napkin ... or, try making your own stamp designs!

Materials

- ❐ Four white napkins
- ❐ Stamp-making supplies (see page 16)
- ❐ Dark red acrylic fabric paint
- ❐ Sponges
- ❐ Paintbrush
- ❐ Tracing paper
- ❐ Pen
- ❐ Paper plate or paint palette
- ❐ Vinyl gloves
- ❐ Plastic sheeting
- ❐ Iron

Instructions

This project is suitable for all skill levels.

1 Copy henna patterns onto tracing paper. Following instructions on page 16, make henna stamps.

2 Fold napkins in half. Fold again in half. Press folded napkin to mark center point and center of each edge.

3 Cover work surface with plastic sheeting.

4 Using paintbrush, place small amount of acrylic paint on paper plate.

5 Using sponge, apply a thin layer of acrylic paint to stamps.

6 Stamp pattern on napkin. Consider stamping in the following positions: centerfold of napkin, in corners and center of each edge.

7 Allow to dry. Set paint following manufacturer's instructions.

Henna napkin designs.

Asian Inspired Hot Plate

Asian trivet.

This striking ceramic trivet combines several different influences in Asian art. Arabic mosaic tile art gave me the interlocking circular design. I took the blue and white color from traditional Chinese blue and white ceramics. Appreciating the beauty of handcrafted everyday articles is recognized in Japan as Mingei. Try your hand at this easy project that captures three diverse traditions.

About Mingei

Mingei is a Japanese word for "folk art," or art of common people. Dr. Yanagi Soetsu, a philosopher and art critic, invented the word in 1925 by combining the Japanese words for "all people" (min) and "art" (gei). Dr. Yanagi and his friends, Hamada Shoji and Kawai Kanjiro, established the folk art movement in Japan in the 1920s.

Before the 20th century, Japan had for centuries enjoyed a vibrant tradition of handmade goods. Artisans made products to meet the needs of the general production. By the late 19th century, however, Japanese craftwork began to disappear as the government encouraged and developed mass production to make goods cheaply and quickly. Concerned with this rapid Western industrialization, Yanagi sought a return to the recognition of the beauty of traditional Japanese craftwork. He observed that many useful, pre-industrial artifacts, made by unknown craftsmen, were of beauty seldom equaled in pieces made with modern industrial techniques.

Through his initiatives, Yanagi re-taught the Japanese to respect and enjoy high quality, traditional handmade crafts of all types: ceramics, wood objects, baskets, textiles, and lacquer products. He not only rescued craft traditions from extinction in Japan, but through his book, The Unknown Craftsman, Yanagi introduced the West to Japan's rich heritage of folk arts. With his friends Hamada and Kanjiro, Yanagi, he founded the Nihon Mingei Kyokai, the Japan Folk Art Association, and published a journal, Mingei, which is still published today. Their famous collection of Mingei objects is on display in their Tokyo museum, the Nihon MingeiKan.

Today, a strong Mingei tradition and movement flourishes in Japan, and is encouraged around the world. (Sources: Mingei International Museum, http://www.Mingei.org; About Mingei, http://www.blueandwhiteamerica.com/Mingei.html; Mingeikan-The Japan Folk Crafts Museum, http://www.Mingeikan.or.jp/Pages/entrance-e.html.)

Materials

- ☐ White ceramic tile, 6" x 6"
- ☐ Dark blue tile paint
- ☐ Vinyl gloves
- ☐ Stencil adhesive spray (optional)
- ☐ Sponges
- ☐ Stencil making supplies (see page 9)
- ☐ Plastic sheeting

Instructions

This project is suitable for all skill levels.
Review manufacturer's instructions for using tile paint. You may require additional supplies based on manufacturer's instructions.

1 Trace and cut stencil (see page 9).

2 Cover work surface with plastic sheeting.

3 Wash and dry ceramic tile.

4 Center stencil on dry tile. Adhere with stencil adhesive spary.

5 Using sponge, stencil pattern onto tile. Allow to dry.

6 Follow manufacturer's instructions for setting paint on tile.

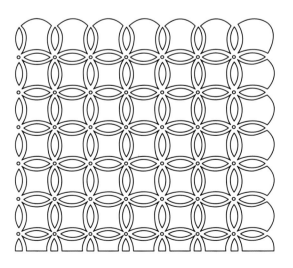

Sashiko Glass Container

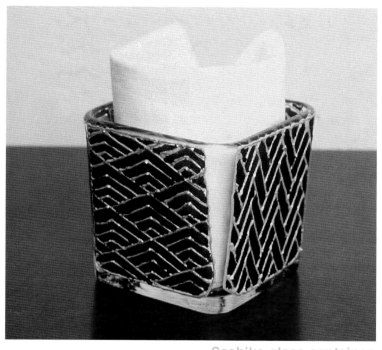

Sashiko glass container.

This beautiful, cobalt blue container is a wonderful place to store your treasures. Easy to make, and very striking-you will only get compliments with this project.

Sashiko

Sashiko is an ancient Japanese quilting art. What was started by Japanese peasants from the simple necessity for patching holes in work clothes has evolved into a stunning art of quilting and embroidery. As peasants had little access to cloth and thread until the 18th century, new garments were rare and saved for special occasions. Working clothes were painstakingly repaired over and over. Originally, patches were stitched over worn areas of clothing using threads in the same color as the garment. Eventually, undyed cotton thread became available. As the white thread made a striking contrast against the indigo-dyed fabrics used in garments, peasants created more striking designs. With the availability of cotton thread, peasants started quilting together multiple layers of fabrics to create warm clothing that could guard against the elements.

By the 19th century, Sashiko was practiced not only for practical purposes but also as decorative art. The merchant classes took note and adopted the art, and Sashiko once-and-for all lost its association with mending and emerged as an artistic medium. Artists created thousands of patterns. Today, the Japanese take great national pride in Sashiko, and practice the art solely for its decorative purposes. (Source: *Sashiko,* Mary S. Parker, Lark Books, 1999.)

Materials

- ❏ Square glass container (or size of your choice), 4" x 4" x 4"
- ❏ Tube of silver glass outliner acrylic paint
- ❏ Blue glass paint (a deep, vibrant color close to indigo blue)
- ❏ Paintbrush
- ❏ Bowl of rinsing water
- ❏ Paper towels
- ❏ Scotch tape
- ❏ Glass cleaner or isopropyl alcohol
- ❏ Vinyl gloves
- ❏ Plastic sheeting

Higaki Cypress fence pattern.

Hishi Seigaiha diamond-shaped waves.

Source: *Sashiko*, Mary S. Parker, Lark Books, 1999.

This pattern represents the design made when cypress slats are woven to make a fence.

Instructions

This project is suitable for all skill levels.
Read manufacturer's instructions for working with glass paint. You may require additional supplies based on manufacturer's instructions.

1. Enlarge pattern 200 percent. Copy and cut out four copies of Sashiko patterns (one for each side of container). You will need to adjust the size of the Sashiko patterns if you use a different size container.

2. Cover work surface with plastic sheeting.

3. Wash and dry glass container. Wipe outside surface with glass cleaner (or alcohol).

4. Tape Sashiko patterns to inside of glass container.

5. Working on the outside of container, draw the lines of Sashiko pattern using silver outliner paint. Allow to dry between sides.

6. Using the paintbrush, work carefully to fill in the spaces between the lines with the blue glass paint. Rinse paintbrush as necessary. Dry the paintbrush on paper towels after rinsing to prevent diluting paint. Continue until all spaces are completely filled with blue paint. Allow to dry.

7. Follow manufacturer's instructions for curing paint if necessary.

Kuba-patterned Container

Kuba Cloth patterned container.

A simple, inexpensive glass jar is trans-formed into something special using the elegant, geometric patterns of appliquéd Kuba cloth.

Kuba Cloth

Kuba cloth is unmistakably one of the most elegant fab-rics in the world. A raffia fabric, made by the Kuba peo-ple of Democratic Republic of Congo, Kuba cloth has been collected and admired by foreigners since the 1600s. This beautiful fabric has inspired ordinary and famous alike, including Pablo Picasso, Henri Matisse, and Paul Klee.

Kuba cloth's appeal is in the rhythm of the design. Abstract, geometric patterns in a limited color palette meander and merge in a soft, fluid, undulating manner. Motifs change; one flows seamlessly into another, and whether by mistake or intent of the designer, nothing seems out of place. Kuba cloth plays with your optical senses. The expected and unexpected appear: motifs recede and proceed, appear and disappear, and wander across the cloth. The basic color palette is narrow (most-ly earth tones), but the Kuba are masters at using these colors to produce exciting tone-on-tone tex-tiles with flashes of color. Kuba cloth is never boring.

Today, Los Angeles County Museum of Art and the National Museum in Belgium house large collections of Kuba cloth. (Source: *African Fabrics. Sewing Contemporary Fashion with Ethnic Flair*, Ronke Luke-Boone, Krause 2001.)

Samples of Kuba cloth.

Materials

- ☐ Square glass container, 4" x 4" x 4"
- ☐ Silver leaf kit
- ☐ Contact paper
- ☐ Tracing paper
- ☐ Transfer paper
- ☐ Pencil
- ☐ Pen
- ☐ Scissors
- ☐ Masking tape
- ☐ Etching cream
- ☐ Craft lollipop stick
- ☐ Vinyl gloves
- ☐ Safety glasses
- ☐ Plastic sheeting
- ☐ Stencil-making supplies (see page 9)

Kuba cloth pattern.

Enlarge stencil to 111%

Instructions

This project is suitable for all skill levels (minors should be supervised and not permitted to apply etching cream and silver leaf). Read through all manufacturers' instructions for working with stencil burner, etching cream and silver leaf before starting. You may need additional supplies based on manufacturer's instructions. Wear safety goggles and vinyl gloves when working with etching cream.

1. Copy Kuba cloth pattern to tracing paper.

2. Cut a section of Contact paper at least ½" larger than the pattern. Using transfer paper, copy pattern to film side of Contact paper. You may have to tape Contact paper to work surface to prevent slipping.

3. Using X-Acto knife or stencil burner, cut out four stencils of Kuba cloth pattern. (See directions in Chapter 1).

4. Wash and dry glass container.

5. Adhere stencils to the outside of glass container.

6. Cover work surface with plastic sheeting.

7. Following manufacturer's instructions, apply etching cream with lollipop stick. Do not apply etching cream beyond the edges of the Contact paper. Wear safety glasses and vinyl gloves when applying etching cream.

8. Allow etching cream to act for the duration specified per manufacturer's instructions.

9. Rinse etching cream. Dry.

10. Follow manufacturer's instructions to apply silver leaf around the rim of the glass container.

Etched Adire Wall Art

Etched Adire art.

Etched shapes on picture frames make a very interesting, subtle piece of wall art.

Design Tip

Don't limit yourself to picture frames. Etch patterns on glass shelves, mirrors, or windowpanes to create unusual and delightful pieces.

Materials

- ❑ Two clip art picture frames, 4" x 6"
- ❑ Sheet of colored paper
- ❑ Etching cream
- ❑ Craft lollipop stick
- ❑ Contact paper
- ❑ Vinyl gloves
- ❑ Safety glasses
- ❑ Stencil making supplies (see page 9)
- ❑ Plastic sheeting
- ❑ Pencil
- ❑ Ruler

Instructions

This project is suitable for all skill levels (minors must be supervised when working with etching cream).
Read through all manufacturer's instructions for working with etching cream before starting. You may need additional supplies based on manufacturer's instructions. Wear safety goggles and vinyl gloves when working with etching cream.

1 Follow instructions on page 9 to make Adire stencils out of Contact paper. Keep cut-outs of Adire shapes after cutting stencil.

2 Cover work surface with plastic sheeting.

3 Wash and dry picture frame glass.

4 Adhere stencils to one glass sheet. Adhere stencil cut-outs to the other sheet.

5 Following manufacturer's instructions, apply etching cream with lollipop stick.

6 Allow etching cream to act for the duration specified per manufacturer's instructions.

7 Rinse etching cream. Dry.

8 Measure and cut two 4" x 6" pieces of colored paper.

9 Place paper under glass and reassemble picture frame.

Mondrian Inspired Mirror

Dutch artist Piet Mondrian's distinct and recognizable grid paintings inspired this cheerful, simple mirror. It adds color and style to any room.

Mondrian mirror.

Piet Mondrian

Piet Mondrian's work is probably among the most recognizable among abstract artists of the 20th century. His minimalist paintings remain fresh and vibrant today. Mondrian used vertical and horizontal black lines that outlined blocks of pure white, red, blue, or yellow to express his conception of ultimate harmony and equilibrium.

Mondrian was born in the Netherlands in 1872. His early paintings were landscapes but, by 1909, he grew increasingly interested in abstract renditions of natural objects. In 1912, he moved to Paris where he was greatly influenced by the work of cubist painters. He was visiting the Netherlands when World War I broke out, and he could not return to Paris. He spent the war years further refining his theory of abstraction. Together with Theo van Doesburg, Bart van der Leck, and Georges Vantongerloo, Mondrian developed the Dutch movement called Neo-Plasticism-a rigid form of abstraction. Neo-Plasticism's rules allow only for a canvas subsected into rectangles by vertical and horizontal lines, colored using a very limited palette.

Some of Mondrian's most famous and easily recognizable works bear simple titles such as "Composition in Red, Yellow and Blue" (1926), and "Composition in White, Black and Red" (1936). With war looming, Mondrian moved to England in 1938 and, following the outbreak of World War II, to New York in 1940. He joined American abstract artists in New York and continued to paint and publish texts on Neo-Plasticism. His work, which evolved in New York in response to the layout of the city, was admired by other artists, but did not sell well to the public at the time. Today it is greatly admired. Mondrian died in New York in 1944. (Sources: Piet Mondrian, www.the-artfile.com/uk/artists/mondriaan/mondriaan.htm, Piet Mondrian Online, www.artcyclopedia.com/artists/mondrian_piet .html, Piet Mondrian, http://www.guggenheimcollection.org/site/artist_bio_112.html, Piet Mondrian http://titan.glo.be/~gd30144/mondrian .html)

Mondrian Inspired Mirror

Materials

- Mirror, 36" x 24"
- Glass paint:
    - Yellow
    - Red
    - Blue
    - White frosted
- Grey/lead color glass paint outliner
- Paintbrush
- Bowl of rinsing water
- Paper towels
- Ruler
- Felt-tip marker
- Isopropyl alcohol or glass cleaner
- Vinyl gloves
- Plastic sheeting

Mondrian mirror patterns.

Enlarge stencil to 130%

Instructions

This project is suitable for all skill levels.
Professional services may be needed to frame mirror. Use glass paint that does not require baking to cure.

1 Cover work surface with plastic sheeting.

2 Clean mirror with glass cleaner. Dry.

3 Using ruler and felt-tip pen, measure and mark 4" squares along the outer edges of the mirror. You will have four squares across to top and bottom edges, and six squares along the right and left edges.

4 Measure and mark grid and square patterns on some of the squares creating a pattern of your choice.

5 Outline the grid and squares with glass outliner paint. Allow to dry according to manufacturer's instructions.

6 Paint the squares as pleasing to you, and grid patterns blue, red, yellow, and frost white. Rinse paintbrush when you change colors. Dry paintbrush using paper towel after rinsing to prevent diluting paints. Allow to dry according to manufacturer's instructions.

7 Frame mirror, or have mirror framed by professional framer.

Mondrian Inspired Hot Plates

P lain white ceramic tiles are transformed into interesting modern art trivets à la Dutch artist Piet Mondrian's distinct style. They are an easy way to add bursts of color to your kitchen or table setting.

Mondrian trivet.

Materials

- Two white ceramic tiles, 6" x 6"
- Glass paints:
  Yellow
  Red
  Blue
- Grey/lead color glass paint outliner
- Paintbrush
- Bowl of rinsing water
- Paper towels
- Ruler
- Felt-tip marker
- Isopropyl alcohol or glass cleaner
- Vinyl gloves
- Plastic sheeting

Instructions

This project is suitable for all skill levels.
Review manufacturer's instructions for using glass paints before beginning. You may require additional supplies based on manufacturer's instructions.

1 Cover work surface with plastic sheeting.

2 Wash and dry tiles.

3 Enlarge Mondrian pattern to size of tiles. (See page 71.)

4 Following measurements on copy of pattern, use the ruler and felt-tip pen to mark the pattern onto ceramic tiles.

5 Outline the grid and squares with glass outliner paint. Allow to dry according to manufacturer's instructions.

6 Paint the squares and grid patterns blue, red, and yellow, as you desire. Rinse paintbrush before starting another color. Dry paintbrush using paper towel after rinsing to prevent diluting paints. Allow paint to dry according to manufacturer's instructions.

7 Cure paint following manufacturer's instructions as necessary.

Paper-covered Gift Boxes

Covered gift boxes.

A pretty gift box heightens the anticipation for the gift inside. With so many great papers available today, these boxes are easy to make.

Materials

- ❏ Plain gift box
- ❏ Decorative paper
- ❏ Spray adhesive
- ❏ All-purpose glue
- ❏ Plastic sheeting or old newspaper
- ❏ Stamps or stencils (optional)
- ❏ Scissors
- ❏ Pencil

Instructions

This project is suitable for all skill levels.

1. Gently pry open side seam of box so it opens flat.

2. Cover work surface (and paper) with plastic sheeting.

3. Lay decorative paper right side down on work surface (wrong side should face up).

4. Spray adhesive on outside surface of opened box.

5. Adhere box to decorative paper. Smooth with hand.

6. Cut out covered box. (Optional: Stamp or stencil designs of your choice onto the surface of box. I used Chinese stamps to decorate the box on the right in picture.)

7. Glue sides of box together again using all-purpose glue. Allow to dry.

Painted Ceramic Door and Drawer Pulls

Ceramic door and drawer pulls.

*P*atterns from Arabic tiles, the Hopi, and Adinkra symbols turn plain white door pulls into cheerful furniture accessories. This a quick, inexpensive way to add a punch of color to doors and drawers anywhere in your home.

Materials

❏ Ceramic pulls
❏ Ceramic paint pens
❏ Vinyl gloves

Instructions

This project is suitable for all skill levels.
Review paint pen manufacturer's instructions before starting. You may require additional supplies based on manufacturer's instructions.

1 Wash and dry ceramic pulls.

2 Using your paint pen, draw outlines of Hopi or Adinkra designs onto each pull as desired. Allow to dry. (See pages 38 and 56.)

3 Fill outlines with contrasting or matching colors as desired. Allow to dry.

4 Set the ceramic paint following the manufacturer's instructions.

Wall Pictures from Cards

Mounted African mask notecard.

Mounted Feng-shui notecard.

f you've always thought that cards and postcards are only meant to be sent to loved ones, think again. They make great pictures when mounted and framed. So next time you find a card you like, but don't have anyone to send it to, consider using it to decorate your home. I liked the cards in this picture, so I used them as a decorations on doors.

Materials

- ❏ Postcard or note card
- ❏ Decorative papers
- ❏ Scissors
- ❏ Picture frame (optional)
- ❏ Decorative stamps (optional)
- ❏ Stencils (optional)
- ❏ Stamp pad in colors of your choice (optional)
- ❏ Glue or tape
- ❏ Mounting adhesive or tape

Instructions

This project is suitable for all skill levels.

1. Glue or tape card closed. You may also cut off the back of card.

2. Arrange card on background of decorative paper that is pleasing to you. Once satisfied with the arrangement, tape or glue in place. Allow to dry.

3. Stamp or stencil patterns of your choice on arrangement. Allow to dry.

4. Frame and mount on surface.

4 | **Natural** Textures

Through time, cultures all around the world have used wood, leather, suede, raffia, clay, precious metals and other natural elements to build and furnish homes, to create everyday and decorative articles, and for personal adornment.

Harmonious blend of natural textures.

Wooden Table Runner

*T*hroughout Southeast Asia, simple and exotic woods are used to make furniture, decorative and functional home accessories, and practical everyday artifacts. Capture a bit of casual, yet exotic Southeast Asian style with this wooden table runner.

Materials

- 20 dowels, 36" x 5/16" (sometimes sold precut)
- Small wooden oval beads to fit between dowels, 150
- 2mm leather lace, 10 yd roll
- Wood varnish or stain
- Paper towels
- Soft cloth for stain
- Drill
- Table clamps
- Wood saw
- Fine grain sandpaper
- Safety goggles
- Ruler
- Pencil
- Vinyl gloves

Wooden table runner.

Instructions

This project requires intermediate skill levels. Not suitable for minors. Knowledge of, and comfort with, using sawing and drilling equipment is necessary for this project. Otherwise, seek professional services to cut and drill dowels.

1 Mark and cut each dowel into three 12"-long pieces.

2 Mark small dots 1" from each end of the cut dowels. Ensure that you mark your dots in the same plane. This will avoid twisting when you thread the dowels together.

3 Secure your dowel in the clamp and drill a hole through the dowel at each marked point.

4 Sand dowels with sandpaper to smooth surface.

5 Apply wood varnish or stain. Use two coats if necessary. Allow to dry.

6 Cut two 3 yd strands of lace. Tie a knot at one end of each strand. String three wood beads onto leather. Tie a knot. String first dowel. Follow with two beads. Then alternate dowels and two wood beads until all (or sufficient) dowels are strung. Tie a knot on the last dowel. Finish with three wooden beads. Tie knots in the ends of the leather lace to secure dowels and beads finish table runner.

Gold Leaf Vase

Gold leaf vase.

This project proves that inspiration comes from everywhere. A ceramic done in the sgraffito process inspired me to create this wooden vase decorated in random irregular, vertical stripes of gold leaf. "Sgraffito" comes from the Italian word "graffiare" that literally means to scratch. In ceramics, artists using the sgraffito process scratch a pattern through two or more layers of colored clay to reveal the layers below and create a pattern in the desired colors. I applied the gold leaf in uneven stripes to mimic primitive scratching.

Instructions

This project is suitable for all skill levels (minors should be supervised when applying gold leaf). Review manufacturer's instructions for applying gold leaf before starting. You may require additional supplies based on manufacturer's instructions.

Materials

- ❏ Wooden vase
- ❏ Gold leaf kit
- ❏ Contact paper
- ❏ Stencil burner or craft knife
- ❏ Transfer paper
- ❏ Pen
- ❏ Scissors
- ❏ Vinyl gloves
- ❏ Plastic sheeting

1 Cover work surface with plastic sheeting.

2 Measure the height of your vase.

3 Photocopy and enlarge pattern to fit vase.

4 Copy pattern to Contact paper using transfer paper.

5 Cut stencil out of Contact paper, following instructions in Chapter 1.

6 Adhere stencil to wooden vase.

Gold leaf vase pattern.

7 Follow manufacturer's instructions for applying gold leaf to wood surface. Allow to dry per manufacturer's instructions.

Adinkra Place Mats

Design Tip

Mark off squares along the short edges of place mats .

Adinkra place mat.

Materials

- ☐ Four cream-colored place mats
- ☐ Fabric paint:
  Bronze
  Gold
  Dark
- ☐ Sponges
- ☐ Paintbrush
- ☐ Stencil burner or craft knife
- ☐ Stencil making supplies (see page 9)
- ☐ Paper plate
- ☐ Paper towels
- ☐ Ruler
- ☐ Marking pen
- ☐ Vinyl gloves
- ☐ Plastic sheeting
- ☐ Stamp-making supplies (see page 14)

Instructions

This project is suitable for all skill levels.

1 Cover work surface with plastic sheeting.

2 Make Adinkra stamps following guidelines on page 14. (See page 38 for Adinkra stamps.)

3 Cut stencil for grid lines following guidelines on page 9. (See page 54 for gridline template.)

4 Measure and mark-off two rows of even-sized squares (or rectangles) along either edge of place mat.

5 Place a small amount of bronze paint on a paper plate. Using grid stencil, stencil grid lines. Allow to dry between applications as necessary.

6 Using sponge, apply thin layer of acrylic paint to Adinkra stamp. Stamp Adinkra patterns within the marked squares in your choice of colors. Continue stamping until all squares filled with stamps in your desired color and patterns. Allow to dry.

7 Follow manufacturer's instructions for curing paint as necessary.

Raffia Napkin Rings

Raffia napkin rings.

*T*hese raffia-wrapped napkin rings are a great way to add a sunny, cheerful climate to your table setting. Best of all, they are so simple to make.

Materials

- ❑ Raffia of different colors
- ❑ Plain wooden napkin rings
- ❑ All purpose glue
- ❑ Sponge brush
- ❑ Paint in colors to match raffia
- ❑ Paintbrush
- ❑ Vinyl gloves
- ❑ Scissors
- ❑ Small binder clips
- ❑ Plastic sheeting or old newspaper

Instructions

This project is suitable for all skill levels.

1 Cover work surface with plastic sheeting or newspaper.

2 Paint inside and outside surfaces of napkin rings. Allow to dry.

3 Cut several 24" strands of raffia.

4 Using sponge brush, apply glue onto outside of napkin ring.

5 Wrap one or more layers of raffia around the ring until wood surface is covered to create a base layer. You will have to hold the start and end of raffia in place for a while until it adheres to surface. Use small binder clips in areas close to the napkin rim to hold start and end of raffia strands. Join strands together with a small knot, or overlap the start of a new strand over an end of the finishing strand.

6 Wrap and tie a bow out of a contrasting strand of raffia. See illustrations at right for other options.

Decorative options for raffia napkin rings.

Hopi Pattern Bowl

Hopi patterned bowl.

Decorative patterns on Hopi pottery inspired the pattern on this bowl. A stencil of a Hopi pattern makes an ordinary bowl more interesting.

Hopi Pottery

Hopi clay is considered the finest clay in the Southwest. The clay, which the Hopi have used for over 600 years, hardens to a strong piece and turns beautiful shades of yellow and orange when fired. The traditional Hopi technique is called Sikyatki, named after the village long abandoned before the Europeans came to America. While archeological records showed that the Hopi, like other Pueblo, were known as skilled potters for centuries. One woman-Nampeyo, a Tewa potter from Hano (in Arizona)-is credited for the revival and development of the modern era of Hopi pottery that started at the end of the 19th century. Nampeyo used Sikyatki techniques to create and decorate beautiful pots that were widely sought after. Well-made Hopi pots are uniform and symmetrical, with walls of even thickness from base to rim. The greater the skill of the potter, the thinner the walls and lighter the pot that was created. (Sources: *Treasures of the Hopi*, Theda Bassman, Northland Publishing, 1997; *Crafts from North American Indian Arts*, Mary Lou Stribling, Crown Publishers, 1975.).

Materials

- ❑ Plain wooden bowl
- ❑ Black acrylic paint
- ❑ Stencil adhesive spray
- ❑ Sponges
- ❑ Ruler
- ❑ Pencil
- ❑ Vinyl gloves
- ❑ Contact paper or transparencies
- ❑ Stencil making supplies (see page 9)
- ❑ Plastic sheeting or old newspaper

Instructions

This project is suitable for all skill levels.

If you make your stencils out of plastic sheets (transparencies), you will need stencil adhesive spray or masking tape to adhere stencil to bowl.

1 Cover work surface with plastic sheeting.

2 Cut stencil of Hopi pattern. (See page 44.)

3 Position and adhere stencil about ¾" below the rim to outside of bowl.

4 Using sponges, stencil the pattern onto the bowl. Allow to dry. You may have to wait for patterns to dry before stenciling the next section of the bowl.

Apache Basket Weave Bowl

An old woven Apache basket with a classic star and flower design inspired the pattern on this bowl. The Apache, like many Native Americans, are skilled basket weavers. While baskets were often made for utilitarian and ceremonial purposes, weavers often integrated decorative patterns into their works that were inspired by nature and traditional tribal symbols. The range of images is endless. Animals, flowers, human figures, and everyday objects are often seen in Apache baskets. These bowls are great for holding fruit, nuts, and other household items.

Apache bowl.

Materials

- ❏ Plain wooden bowl
- ❏ Acrylic paint (I used Nova Color 149 Transparent Red Iron Oxide)
- ❏ Sponges
- ❏ Vinyl gloves
- ❏ Contact paper
- ❏ Stencil making supplies (see page 9)
- ❏ Plastic sheeting or old newspaper

Instructions

This project is suitable for all skill levels.

If you make your stencils out of plastic sheets (transparencies), you will need stencil adhesive spray or masking tape to adhere stencil to bowl.

1 Cover work surface with plastic sheeting.

2 Cut stencil of basket weave and Apache flower out of Contact paper (see page 9).

3 Adhere the stencil to the outside of the bowl.

4 Using sponges, stencil the pattern onto the bowl. Allow to dry. You may have to wait for patterns to dry between stenciling patterns.

Apache flower stencil.

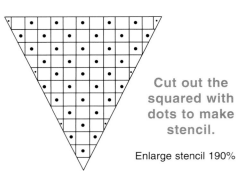

Cut out the squared with dots to make stencil.

Enlarge stencil 190%

5 | **Asian**
Accents

Asian décor and design are admired and have great appeal around the world. It's easy to add Chinese and Japanese elements to your décor with these projects.

Chinese and Japanese inspired accessories.

Bamboo Place Mats

Bamboo place mat.

Add an elegant Asian touch to your place settings with this simple-to-make bamboo place mat.

Materials

- ☐ Red place mats
- ☐ Off-white light weight linen, cotton, or muslin, 1 yd
- ☐ Fabric paints:
  Light green
  Medium green
  Dark green
  Gold
  Red
- ☐ Stencil sponges
- ☐ Stencil adhesive (optional)
- ☐ Fusible web (e.g., Stitch Witchery®)
- ☐ Iron
- ☐ Tape measure
- ☐ Ruler
- ☐ Marking pencil
- ☐ Plastic sheeting
- ☐ Vinyl gloves
- ☐ Stencil making supplies (see page 9, or use purchased bamboo stencil)

A Symbol of Good Fortune

Bamboo has been a symbol of good fortune in Asian culture for over 4000 years. There are many bamboo varieties, including one called "Lucky Bamboo." Throughout Japan, China, and other Asian countries, bamboo is used for decoration and is an important raw material for producing goods. But it is bamboo's ability to adapt and grow anywhere, even in minimal soil and poor light conditions, that ancient culture associated with good fortune. Ancient Asian cultural tradition believes that specific numbers of stalks enhance certain positive aspects of life:

- ■ Three stalks attract happiness
- ■ Five stalks attract wealth
- ■ Seven stalks result in good health
- ■ Twenty-one stalks offer a very powerful all-purpose blessing

Bamboo Place Mats

Bamboo place mat stencil.

Instructions

This project is suitable for all skill levels. You can use purchased bamboo stencils or stamps instead of making them.

1 Cut bamboo stencil following instructions on page 9.

2 Measure the length of your place mat. Divide the length by four and note this measurement. Add 1" to the noted measurement. This is the panel width.

3 Measure the height of your place mat. Add 1" to this measurement. Note the final measurement This is the panel length.

4 Out of your fabric, measure, mark, and cut one piece equivalent to the final length and width measurements in Steps 2 and 3. Cut a piece for each of your place mats.

5 Cover work surface with plastic sheeting.

6 Stencil bamboo onto cotton. Vary the shades of green you use. Add hints of gold and red for interest. Overlap bamboo stalks as you stencil. Allow to dry between stenciling as necessary. Follow manufacturer's instructions for setting paint.

7 Turn under and press ½" seams around the edges of cotton panel cut in Step 4. The panel should be the same height as your place mats.

8 Cut a piece of fusible web to exactly the size of the cotton panel.

9 Position cotton panel at one end of place mat. Insert fusible web underneath the cotton panel. Following manufacturer's instructions, fuse panel to the place mat.

Chinese Decoupage Planter

A *Chinese print decoupage glass container makes a perfect planter for your bamboo plant. This is a simple-to-make project that adds a personal touch to your favorite plant.*

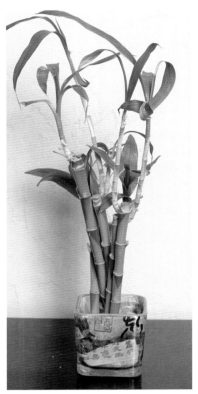

Chinese decoupage planter.

Closeup of Chinese decoupage planter.

Materials

- ❐ Clear glass container, 4" x 4" x 4"
- ❐ Chinese symbol stamp (I purchased a Chinese calligraphy stamp, but it can be handmade)
- ❐ Gold glass paint
- ❐ Red paint stamp pad
- ❐ Clear or contrasting embossing powder
- ❐ Embossing heat tool
- ❐ Decoupage medium
- ❐ Chinese print decorative paper
- ❐ Writing paper (choose color that matches decorative paper)
- ❐ Sponge brushes
- ❐ Paintbrush
- ❐ Vinyl gloves
- ❐ Plastic sheeting

Instructions

This project is suitable for all skill levels
(minors may need assistance with curing glass paint). Review manufacturer's instructions for using glass paint and embossing powder. You may need additional supplies based on manufacturer's instructions.

1 Cover work surface with plastic sheeting.

2 Wash and dry glass container.

3 Paint the rim of the container gold. Allow to dry. Follow manufacturer's instructions for curing paint as necessary.

4 Randomly stamp Chinese symbols over entire surface of writing paper. Emboss with heat tool and embossing powder.

5 Tear the stamped sheet and the decorative paper into small pieces (Chinese characters should still be visible).

6 Using sponge brush, adhere the paper to the glass with decoupage medium. Right side of paper should face glass. Continue until glass surface is completely covered. Allow to dry

Shoji Votive Lantern

Shoji votive lantern.

Japanese Shoji screens are the inspiration for this simple candle votive lantern. Place this Shoji-inspired lantern over a candle votive to create a warm, peaceful environment.

Shoji Screens

Shoji doors, windows, and screens epitomize Japanese design—a style that strives for balance among simplicity, functionality, and beauty. Traditional Japanese shoji screens are made of rice paper, which is applied to a wood lattice with rice glue. The screens provide privacy, yet are subtly translucent and let light into a space. The Japanese replace the rice paper once a year at the New Year. Today, Japanese shoji screens are very popular in the West. They add an elegant touch to any decor.

Materials

- ❏ Waxed paper, 12" wide
- ❏ Piece balsa wood, $\frac{1}{16}$" x 6" x 36"
- ❏ Dark brown wood stain
- ❏ Sponges
- ❏ Vinyl gloves
- ❏ Scissors
- ❏ Craft knife
- ❏ Pencil
- ❏ Ruler
- ❏ Wood glue
- ❏ All purpose glue
- ❏ Double sided clear tape
- ❏ Iron

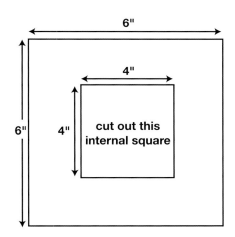

Balsa wood dimensions.

Shoji Votive Lantern

Instructions

This project is suitable for all skill levels.
You may use double-sided tape instead of glue in Step 16.

1 Tear off a 20" length of waxed paper from the roll.

2 Fold in half lengthwise, matching straight edges to create a piece 6" wide. Press with moderately hot iron to fuse sheets together.

3 Measure and cut a 6" x 17" piece out of the length of fused waxed paper.

4 Mark ½" flap lines along all edges of waxed paper.

5 Measure and mark vertical lines at 4" intervals starting to measure from the ½" flap line. Mark horizontal line 3" from the top at center of waxed paper running the whole length of the paper.

6 Fold waxed paper along vertical lines.

7 Measure and mark additional vertical lines 2" from the verticals drawn in Step 5. End these vertical lines at the flap line.

8 Cut 2 strips of waxed paper 1/4" x 16". Center and glue strip over ½" horizontal seam lines that run the length at top and bottom of waxed paper. Allow to dry. These narrow strips will reinforce the fold lines.

9 Cut away the shaded corners of the waxed paper. Carefully cut folds along vertical lines to the top of the horizontal line. Do NOT cut through the horizontal line. Fold along 1/2" seams to make flaps.

10 Measure and cut two squares (6" x 6") out of balsa wood. Measure and mark the center point of both pieces.

11 Measure and mark a 4" square on the inside of the balsa wood squares.

12 Using craft knife, cut out the inner square.

13 Measure and cut four strips of ¼" x 4", and eight strips of ¼" x 3" of balsa wood.

14 Stain front and edges of balsa wood sections dark brown. Allow to dry.

15 Working on the right side of waxed paper, glue ¼" balsa wood strips to waxed paper over pencil markings to form grid. Be careful that the wood strips to do not extend beyond or impede vertical folds.

16 Glue the two ½" flaps A and B together to form a rectangular waxed paper box.

17 Place strips of double-sided tape on the outside of the top flaps of the box and adhere to the underside of the top square wood piece. Stained wood surface should face you.

18 Insert box into the bottom square. Use double sided tape to adhere flaps of box to the underside of the bottom wood square. Stained side should face you.

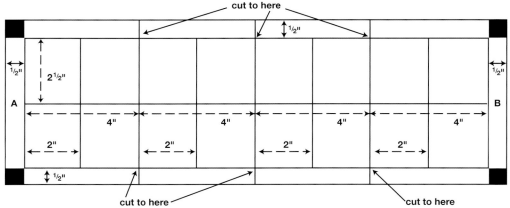

Waxed paper dimensions.

Chinese Calligraphy Votive

Chinese symbols votive.

Materials

- ☐ Clear glass votive
- ☐ Glass etching cream
- ☐ Craft lollipop stick
- ☐ Plastic sheeting
- ☐ Safety glasses
- ☐ Vinyl gloves
- ☐ Contact paper
- ☐ Stencil-making supplies
  (see pages 9)

With Chinese symbols for peace, friendship, peace, happiness, and eternity, a simple votive conveys a wonderful message while creating a warm atmosphere.

Design Tip

Etch other symbols of your choice onto your votives. Try any of the other symbols in this book-Hopi, Adire, Adinkra, Kuba, Sashiko.

Instructions

This project is suitable for all skill levels

(minors should be supervised when working with etching cream). Review manufacturer's instructions for using etching cream before starting. You may require additional supplies based on manufacturer's instructions. Wear safety glasses and vinyl gloves when working with etching cream.

1 Make stencils of Chinese symbols for good luck, peace, eternity, friendship, and happiness out of Contact paper following instructions on page 9.

2 Cut stencils out of Contact paper so that there is at least 1" around the symbol.

3 Wash and dry glass votive.

4 Working one stencil at a time, adhere the stencil to the outside of glass votive.

5 Following manufacturer's instructions, use etching cream to etch symbol onto glass. Rinse and dry.

6 Position next stencil at desired position.

7 Repeat Steps 4 and 5 until you complete etching all the symbols.

8 Rinse votive according to manufacturer's directions.

joy

spirit

eternity

wisdom

happiness

good luck

dream

god

friendship

peace

tranquility

courage

Chinese "Peace" and "Good Luck" Tiles

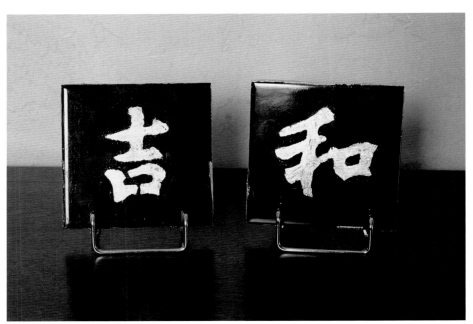

Chinese symbols for peace and good luck expressed in gold leaf makes beautiful art. They are simple to make, and you have endless choices of Chinese symbols to express yourself.

Chinese Peace and Good Luck tiles.

Chinese Writing

Don't look for a Chinese alphabet-it doesn't exist. Unlike the Greek alphabet that consists of letters with phonetic sound, the Chinese writing system is based on symbols that have sounds and represent concepts. Compared to most alphabets that have 20 to 50 letters, there are thousands of symbols in the Chinese writing system. Small dictionaries have at least 6,000 symbols, while larger ones can have as many as 40,000 to 50,000 symbols. In general, 6,000 symbols are essential for everyday use, and knowledge of about 3,000 symbols is necessary to read a newspaper. China's writing system is centuries old. The earliest example of Chinese writing dates back to 1200 B.C.

Like Arabic, Chinese symbols have become vehicles of art. Calligraphy, once an important skill and discipline of the Chinese literary intelligentsia, is still widely practiced today. (Source: Logoi.com-The Online Language Source, http://www.logoi.com/.)

Chinese "Peace" and "Good Luck" Tiles

Materials

- [ ] Two cobalt blue ceramic tiles, 4" x 4"
- [ ] Gold leaf kit
- [ ] Paper
- [ ] Vinyl gloves
- [ ] Ceramic varnish
- [ ] Stencil adhesive spray (optional)
- [ ] Stencil making supplies (see page 9)
- [ ] Plastic sheeting

peace

good luck

Instructions

This project is suitable for all skill levels

(minors must be supervised when working with gold leaf). Review manufacturer's instructions for using gold leaf before starting. You may require additional supplies based on manufacturer's instructions.

1 Make enlarged copies of Chinese symbols of your choice. Enlarge symbols to about 3" height. I used symbols for "peace" and "good luck."

2 Cut stencil of symbol (see page 9).

3 Cover work surface with plastic sheeting.

4 Wash and dry ceramic tile.

5 Center and adhere stencil on dry tile.

6 Follow manufacturer's instructions to apply gold leaf to tile through stencil.

7 Remove stencil. Complete applying gold leaf following manufacturer's instructions. Allow gold leaf application to dry.

8 Apply gold leaf around four edges of tile. Allow gold leaf application to dry.

9 Seal tile with two coats of varnish. Allow varnish to dry between coats.

6 | **Pretty** Powder Room

Handmade soap, pretty tiles, embroidered towels, and pretty accessories make this room delightful.

Arabic-inspired Ceramic Tiles

Arabic tiles.

T hroughout North Africa and the Middle East, there is a long tradition of ceramic arts. Skilled artists make exquisite tiles and ceramic ware with intricate patterns and sophisticated colors that have inspired and awed many throughout the years. Add a sparkle to any kitchen or bath with an exotic back splash or wall tiles.

Materials

- ❏ Four white ceramic tiles, 4" x 4" (adjust stencil size if different sized tile used)
- ❏ Ceramic paint:
    - Blue
    - Yellow (or colors of your choice)
- ❏ Ceramic paint pens:
    - Blue
    - Yellow
    - Red (or colors of your choice)
- ❏ Stencil making supplies (see page 9)
- ❏ Stencil sponges
- ❏ Sponge brush
- ❏ Vinyl gloves
- ❏ Masking tape
- ❏ Ceramic tile varnish
- ❏ Stencil spray adhesive
- ❏ Plastic sheeting

Design Tip

Use exotic tiles as trivets for serving or as a centerpiece on a kitchen table.

Enlarge stencils 133%

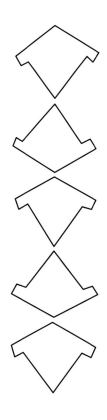

Arabic-inspired Ceramic Tiles

Islamic and Arabic Tiles

We probably have the Babylonians and Assyrians to thank for inventing tiles. Archeology shows that they made and decorated the facades of their homes with glazed bricks as early as 9000 B.C. But it was ancient Egyptians who invented glazed tiles. Records show Egyptian potters made clear blue and green tiles about 4000 B.C. From Egypt, the art of glazing tiles spread throughout the Islamic world. Potters in Egypt, Syria, Persia, Palestine, and Mesopotamia invented new techniques and traditions for making and glazing tiles. For example, glazes containing particles of gold and silver that, when fired on tiles, produced a sparkling iridescent effect, were invented in the 11th century. Islamic architecture and aesthetic favored decorating surfaces with tiles arranged in dazzling, elaborate, and complex geometric patterns. Small tiles were arranged to create complicated interlocking patterns that were used to decorate buildings. Walls, floors, and ceilings were equal candidates for decoration. The Moors brought Islam and their ceramic skills with them to Spain, from where Islamic decorative skills and techniques spread into and throughout Europe. The Great Mosque of Damascus, built between A.D. 805-15, and Alhambra Palace in Granada, Spain, are wonderful examples of ancient and modern Islamic tile. (Sources: *Cultures of the World*, Morocco, Pat Seward, Marshall Cavendish, 1995; Pattern Design, Lewis F. Day, Dover Press, New York, 1999; *The Tile Decorating Book, Decorating and Hand-painting Tiles - A Practical Guide*, Marion Elliot, Lorenz Books, 1997.)

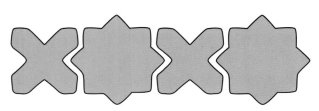

Enlarge stencil 125%

Instructions

This project is suitable for all skill levels.
Cover work surface with plastic sheeting before starting any of the following projects. Review manufacturer's instructions for using tile paints. You may require additional supplies based on manufacturer's instructions.

Repeating Pattern Tiles (bottom left and top right)

1 Follow paint manufacturer's instructions to prepare tiles for decoration.

2 Cut tile stencil following directions on page 9. Adhere stencil to tile using stencil adhesive.

3 Use stencil sponges to stencil pattern over tile. Continue to stencil pattern until entire tile surface is covered. Allow paint to dry. You may need to wait until paint is dry before stenciling the next row.

4 Outline each shape in contrasting colors using paint pens.

5 Place a single red dot in the center of the yellow shapes. Allow to dry.

6 Follow manufacturer's instructions to set paint as necessary.

7 Seal the surface of the tile with two coats of ceramic varnish. Allow to dry between coats.

Swirling Pattern Tiles (bottom right and top left)

8 Lightly stroke a yellow paint base on tile with sponge brush. Wipe off excess.

9 Follow Steps 1 through 3. Allow to dry.

10 Place a single red dot at the ends and center of swirls as desired. Allow to dry.

11 Follow manufacturer's instructions to set paint as necessary.

Handmade Soap

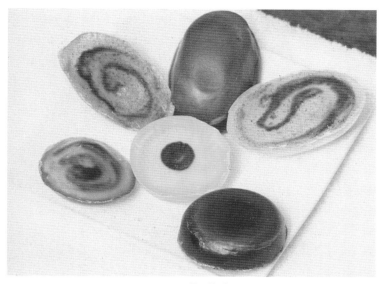

Delicious" handmade soap.

Pamper yourself with hand-made bars of soap, or give them as gifts to your loved ones. These bars will fool everyone, as they look good enough to eat. They are simple, fun, and easy to make.

Materials

- ❏ Glycerin bar
- ❏ Glass bowl
- ❏ Fragrance
- ❏ Color
- ❏ Purchased soap molds
- ❏ Microwave
- ❏ Measuring jug (microwave safe)
- ❏ Wooden spatula

Instructions

This project is suitable for all skill levels (minors should be supervised as melted glycerin is hot).

1 Place desired amount of glycerin into glass bowl. Heat in microwave until all is melted. Caution-melted glycerin is hot!

2 Add color and fragrance as desired. Stir. Small drops of color are sufficient for vibrantly-colored soap.

3 Pour liquid glycerin into molds and allow to cool. Soap will harden as it cools.

4 Gently push soap out of mold once hardened.

Fragrances

Humans have always loved fragrances. Throughout history, perfumes, essential oils, and scents have been associated with mood, love, health, healing, religion, ritual, and much of everyday human life. Perfumes and essential oils have been shown to have certain benefits. Here are some properties of popular oils and scents. Consider these as you personalize your soap:

- ■ Chamomile-very soothing, gentle essential oil.
- ■ Cinnamon-warm, spicy aroma. Believed to have therapeutic benefits.
- ■ Cloves-distinct, spicy fragrance. Has antiseptic benefits, traditionally used to relieve toothache.
- ■ Lemon-fresh, tangy aroma. Has medicinal properties.
- ■ Orange-sweet, warm, cheerful, uplifting fragrance and properties.
- ■ Peppermint-fresh, cooling fragrance. Refreshing for fatigue. Believed to clear headache.
- ■ Rose-considered the queen of all flower oils. Sensual, feminine fragrance.

(Source: *Heaven Scent, Aromatic Gifts to Make, Send, and Keep*, Labeena Ishaque, Watson-Guptill Publications, 1998.)

Adinkra Towels

Adinkra towels.

Add messages to towels using Adinkra symbols for a decorative touch. This is a very simple project to create wonderful pieces for your home or as gifts for friends or family.

Design Tip

Embroider Adinkra or Hopi symbols to bed linen or even clothing.

Materials

- ❏ Purchased towels
- ❏ Contrasting embroidery thread
- ❏ Scissors
- ❏ Tape measure
- ❏ Tracing paper
- ❏ Pencil
- ❏ Washable marking pen or pencil
- ❏ Programmable embroidery sewing machine or
- ❏ Embroidery hoop and supplies (if embroidering towels yourself)

Instructions

This project requires beginning sewing skills. To make these towels, you must either have a programmable embroidery machine, or you must take the pillow front to a commercial shop to be embroidered. Refer to your machine handbook for a list of other supplies that you require for embroidery. Disregard this step if a commercial service will embroider your pillow.

1 Trace Adinkra symbol. (See page 38.)

2 Photocopy and increase Adinkra motif to desired size.

3 Follow sewing machine instructions and program Adinkra patterns for embroidery. Skip to Step 4 if using a commercial embroidery service.

4 Measure and mark desired position for patterns on towels.

5 Embroider patterns onto towels or take to commercial service for embroidery.

Paisley Bottle

Paisley bottle.

*P*retty bottles are wonderful accents in any room. Here's a simple project for you to make.

Materials

- ❑ Clear or colored glass bottle
- ❑ Blue glass paint
- ❑ Blue felt-tip pen
- ❑ Sponges
- ❑ Silver leaf kit
- ❑ Tracing paper
- ❑ Transfer paper
- ❑ Scotch® tape
- ❑ Pencil
- ❑ Vinyl gloves
- ❑ Plastic sheeting

1 Wash and dry glass bottle.

2 Cover work surface with plastic sheeting.

3 Sponge paint bottle until entire surface is covered. Allow to dry. Cure paint according to manufacturer's instructions. Skip this step is using colored bottle.

4 Apply silver leaf size in small area roughly 1½" square on bottle. Note: Edges of area do not have to be even. Allow to dry.

5 Adhere and smooth silver leaf to bottle over size. Brush away excess leaf.

6 Apply sealer over silver leaf. Allow to dry.

7 Trace paisley design onto tracing paper. Tape transfer paper to the bottle over the silver leaf. Be careful that Scotch tape does not stick to silver leaf. Tape paisley design over transfer paper. Copy paisley design onto bottle.

Paisley design.

8 Using felt-tip pen, copy paisley design you traced onto bottle. Alternatively, skip Step 7 and free-hand a paisley design onto the bottle. Be sure to practice free-hand drawing the paisley design before trying it on the bottle. Allow to dry.

Instructions

This project is suitable for all skill levels (minors should be supervised when working with silver leaf). If you use a colored bottle, you will not require glass paint and sponges; skip Step 3. Review manufacturer's instructions for using glass paint and silver leaf before starting. You may require additional supplies based on manufacturer's instructions.

7 | Around the World
While You Work

Spur your creativity by decorating your workspace with accessories from around the world. A corkboard inspired by Moroccan tile work, a richly-covered notebook, raffia-wrapped containers, and personalized stationery are just a few accessories that are easy to make and look great in your home or work space.

Desk accessories from around the world.

Moroccan Tile Corkboard

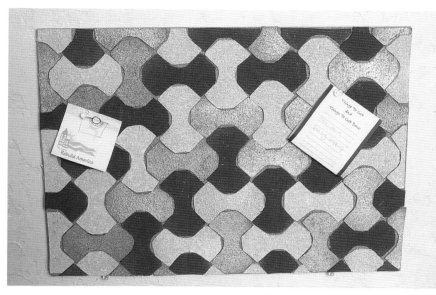

Moroccan tile cork board.

W *hy use a boring cork-board for keeping track of your notes and messages? This Moroccan tile corkboard will add pizzazz to any office space or family message center.*

Instructions

This project is suitable for all skill levels.

1 Cut one sheet of cork (12" x 18") to fit the foam board.

2 Glue cork sheet to foam board. Allow to dry.

3 Trace the template of the Moroccan tile and transfer to poster-board.

4 Cut out tile template.

5 Using template, outline and cut out 45 cork tiles.

6 Divide tiles into three groups of 15 tiles. When using spray paints, work outside and cover work surface with newspaper. Spray paint first group white, second group gold and third group gold. Allow to dry.

7 Starting at one corner of the matt board, glue tiles in place, alternating colors and interlocking tiles as is pleasing to you. You may need to hold tiles in place with weights until the cork adheres and glue dries.

8 Cover entire surface with painted cork tiles. At corners, you will have to trim tiles with scissors to fit the spaces. Allow to dry.

9 On back of foam board, adhere wall mounting adhesive. Mount corkboard to the wall.

Materials

- [ ] Foam board, 12" x 18" or other size you desire
- [ ] Roll of cork, at least 2 yds long
- [ ] Spray paints:
  Red
  Gold
  White
- [ ] Glue (suitable for cork)
- [ ] Tracing paper
- [ ] Posterboard, 12" x 18"
- [ ] Old newspaper
- [ ] Scissors
- [ ] Weights (or soup cans)
- [ ] Pencil
- [ ] Pen
- [ ] Ruler
- [ ] Wall mounting adhesive or hook & loop tape

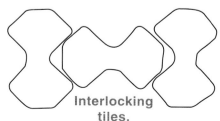

Interlocking tiles.
Enlarge stencil 125%

Indian Spice Paisley Notebook

Capture your thoughts in a pretty notebook. Beautiful handmade paper turns a plain book into a treasure.

Indian spice paisley notebook.

Paisley: The Quest to Capture a Kashmiri Art

It took centuries of conquering armies, global trade, technology, and fashion whimsy to transform the art of the Persians into the generic pattern we call paisley today. Persians brought to India and Kashmir their great art and textile traditions that featured exquisite, intricate floral patterns. Over time, Kashmir transformed and incorporated the Persian aesthetic into their art, creating their motifs, which were woven into fine shawls. One of the patterns was a curled, feather-like, plumed motif called a boteh. It is this motif that evolved into the paisley.

Kashmiri men wore exquisite shawls featuring the boteh and other motifs as turbans, waistbands, scarves, or shoulder mantles. British officials and traders who came to the region took these beautiful shawls back to Britain, and their British women admired them! They were more spectacular than textiles available at the time. Kashmiri shawls became the perfect accessory and were highly coveted by

women in Britain, across Western Europe and the United States. Demand exceeded supply and British weavers started producing imitation shawls in Norwich and Edinburgh, Scotland. It was the small Scottish town-Paisley-that gave its name to the imitation shawls when weavers there vied for a share of the lucrative Kashmiri shawl market.

Kashmiri shawls became a vital element of French fashion at the end of the 18th century. Empress Josephine was said to own hundreds. But the high cost of the shawls led the French to develop the technology to produce a high-quality imitation shawl. At first, the French followed the strict designs of Kashmiri tradition. Slowly, they introduced their changes to the designs. French shawls were soon recognized as superior to the British shawls. British weavers took note. With competition, British and French weavers created their interpretations of traditional Kashmiri designs. Manufacturers eager to find

Indian Spice Paisley Notebook

even cheaper methods to produce shawls started printing patterns on fabric. Suddenly cheap imitations of the once rare and expensive Kashmiri shawl were available everywhere. The paisley shawl became a vulgar imitation. True to its fickle nature, fashion moved on, and by 1870, fashionable women had discarded the paisley shawl. Although paisley shawls are still woven in Europe and the United States, the most common use of woven paisleys is for home furnishings. (Sources: *TextileStyle*, Caroline Clifton-Mogg, Bulfinch Press, 2000; "The History of Paisley," *Fiber Arts Magazine*, Nov./Dec., 1997.)

Materials

- ❏ Notebook, 6" x 8½"
- ❏ Thin batting
- ❏ Orange paper
- ❏ Orange & gold paper
- ❏ Purchased paisley stamp
  (I used one from All Night
  Media®)
- ❏ Gold acrylic paint
- ❏ Gold embossing powder
- ❏ Embossing heat tool
- ❏ Sponge
- ❏ Sponge brush
- ❏ All-purpose glue
- ❏ Spray adhesive (optional)
- ❏ Scissors
- ❏ Spray adhesive
- ❏ Ruler
- ❏ Tape measure
- ❏ Old newspaper or plastic
  sheeting (optional)

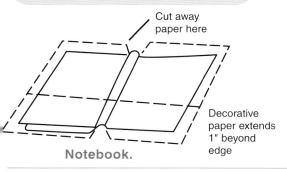

Cut away paper here

Decorative paper extends 1" beyond edge

Notebook.

Instructions

This project is suitable for all skill levels.
Review manufacturer's instructions for using embossing with powder. Adjust measurements given in instructions if you are covering a different size notebook.

1 Measure and cut two pieces of batting to fit the front and back covers of notebook.

2 Glue batting to front and back covers. Use sponge brush to smooth glue before adhering batting. Allow to dry. Rinse sponge brush after use.

3 Measure and cut a 7" x 14½" piece of orange paper. Measure and cut a piece a 4" x 14½" piece of orange/gold paper.

4 Cover work surface with plastic sheeting (if working with spray adhesive).

5 Open and lay book flat on work surface (batting should face you). Position and glue orange paper over upper portion of book cover so that paper extends 1" around all edges (see illustration).

6 Position and glue orange/gold paper over lower portion of book cover so that paper overlaps orange paper and extends 1" around all edges. Allow to dry.

7 Cut away paper at spine of book. Turn over 1" paper flaps and glue inside book cover. Allow to dry (see illustration).

8 Cut a 2" x 3½" piece gold/orange paper. Paint edge of paper gold. Apply small layer of gold paint to stamp using sponges. Stamp paisley pattern in center of the wrong side of paper (plain orange side). Apply gold embossing powder to wet stamp. Use embossing heat tool to dry stamp.

9 Position and glue paisley section on center of book front cover. Allow to dry.

Seminole Lampshade

Seminole shade.

This adorable lampshade is *"quilted" using decorative paper in the traditional Seminole technique. The result is a very interesting, sophisticated lampshade that will get plenty of compliments.*

Seminole Piecework

What started out of necessity, probably in the 1800s, evolved into an intricate geometric pieced art form that is widely admired and recognized today. Seminole piecework consists of teeny-tiny cotton squares arranged in intricate geometric patterns.

Before industrialization, cotton fabrics were quite expensive. Seminole women, probably out of the thrifty need not to waste fabric, joined together small and remnant pieces of cotton into larger strips that were used in clothing. Women wear full-length skirts out of alternating bands of piecework and cotton, with blouses bordered in piecework. Men wear pants and shirts that are bordered with piecework bands.

Once Seminole women had access to sewing machines, they joined together very tiny pieces and their designs became more elaborate and complex. The genius in the Seminole piecework is the simple techniques that were used to make complex geometric designs of small offset squares. The women make a wide range of geometric designs including patterns named "Milky Way," "Alligator Tracks," "Snake Jaw," "Four Crossed Logs," and "Everlasting Fire." Today, the Seminole still wear clothing decorated with piecework for special occasions.

Seminole piecework is now quite popular in quilting throughout the United States. Modern quilters avidly use the strip-piecing techniques Seminole women developed to minimize sewing time.

Materials

- Three sheets of matching or contrasting decorative paper, 30" length each
- Transparent lampshade lining
- All purpose glue
- Top ring, 5" diameter
- Bottom ring, 5" diameter
- Mini clothespins
- Pencil
- Ruler
- Scissors
- Compass (to draw circle)
- Craft knife
- Lamp

Seminole Lampshade

Instructions

This project is suitable for all skill levels (minors may need assistance measuring and gluing small pieces together). The measurements given below are for a 5" diameter shade. Adjust your measurements for shades of different sizes. Consult with a lampshade supply company for basic rings and other hardware you require. See Resources, page 125.

1 **Out of first decorative paper, measure, mark, and cut:**
One 1¼" strip the entire length of paper
One circle 4" diameter

Out of second decorative paper, measure, mark, and cut:

Two 1¼" strips the entire length of paper
One rectangle 5" x 17"
A circle of 5" outer diameter, with inner cut out 3" center. See illustration. (Tip: Use the bottom ring to trace the outer circle.)

Out of third decorative paper, measure, mark and cut a 1" strip the entire length of paper

Out of lampshade lining cut:
One piece 5" x 17"
One circle of 5" outer diameter, with inner cut out 3" center. See illustration.

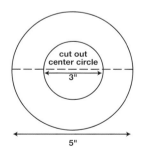

Cutting center circle out of lining and decorative paper.

2 Along the length of one edge of each strip, measure and mark a line ¼" from the edge. Fold the strips along this line toward wrong side of paper. You will create a little flap.

3 Using all-purpose glue, glue the strips of decorating paper together to make a striped band by overlapping the ¼" fold along the length of another strip. Allow to dry.

4 Along the length of strip, mark vertical lines at 1½" intervals. Cut along marked lines.

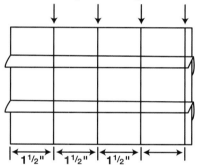

Mark and cut panel along these lines

5 Measure and mark a line ¼" from one vertical edge of each of the cut pieces. Fold paper to wrong side along each marked line, creating a little flap.

6 Glue the little pieces together along the ¼" lines so the pattern is offset one band downward. The stripes will form a diagonally-stepped design. Make sure the corners of the boxes are properly matched. Continue gluing together the pieces until you have a panel long enough for your frame.

Glue strips of decorative paper together.

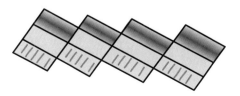

Joining pieces to make stepped Seminole pattern.

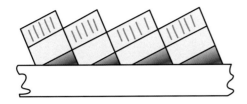

Join strip to make Seminole strip.

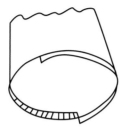

Glue lining to rings. (See Step 9.)

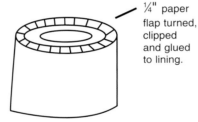

¼" paper flap turned, clipped and glued to lining.

Joining decorative paper to shade lining. See Step 13.

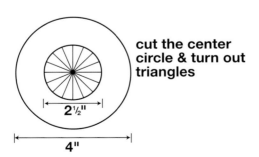

cut the center circle & turn out triangles

2½"

4"

Center circle out of decorative paper.

7 With the right side of the quilted paper panel facing you, position the remaining strip cut from the second decorative paper over the bottom of the panel so that the strip touches the bottom of the second row of squares on the panel. Use all-purpose glue to secure in place.

8 On lampshade lining, mark a line ¼" from top and bottom.

9 Join the top ring to the lamp lining, by folding and gluing the lining over the ring along the ¼" line. Clip the flap with scissors to help fold over ring. Hold in place with clamps if necessary. Allow to dry.

10 Join the bottom ring to the lampshade lining by repeating Step 9.

11 Repeat Step 8, on the 5" x 17" piece you cut out of the second decorative sheet. Glue this decorative sheet over the lampshade lining around the bottom ring by following instructions in Step 9.

12 Position lining circle to top of shade.

13 Attach the lining circle to top of the shade by folding and gluing the ¼" paper flap over the circle. Clip flap with scissors to help turn over and around curves. Allow to dry.

14 Glue the 5" circle (out of second decorative paper) at the top of shade to cover the lining and glued flaps. Allow to dry.

15 On the wrong side of the remaining 4" circle (out of 1st decorative paper), mark and cut the paper starting at center as shown in illustration. Be careful not to cut paper beyond 1-1/4" from the center. Center and glue the circle over the top of lampshade. Allow to dry. Turn the cut center sections outward.

Handmade Thai-paper Box

Handmade Thai-paper box.

Handmade hemp and decorative papers from Thailand give this box its elegant charm.

Materials

- [ ] Handmade Thai papers in matching or contrasting colors
- [ ] Foam board
- [ ] Sealer
- [ ] Decoupage medium
- [ ] Sponge brushes
- [ ] Ruler
- [ ] Pencil
- [ ] Hot glue gun
- [ ] Glue
- [ ] Weights (or cans of soup)
- [ ] Vinyl gloves
- [ ] Plastic sheeting

Instructions

This project is suitable for all skill levels.

1 Cover work surface with plastic sheeting.

2 Using foam brush, apply sealer to foam board. Allow to dry.

3 **Out of foam board, measure, mark, and cut out:**
Two pieces, 2½" x 6"
Two pieces, 2½" x 8"
One piece, 6" x 8½"

4 Arrange the smaller pieces of foam board into a 6" x 8½" rectangle. Glue the ends together with hot glue gun.

5 Tear off pieces of decorative paper. Irregular sections are best.

6 Using sponge brush and decoupage medium, adhere the paper to foam board rectangle and 6" x 8½" piece. Overlap paper as you desire. Allow to dry.

7 Glue rectangle sides to 6" x 8½" base. Hold in place using weights while glue dries.

Nepalese/Tibetan-paper Covered Magazine Holders

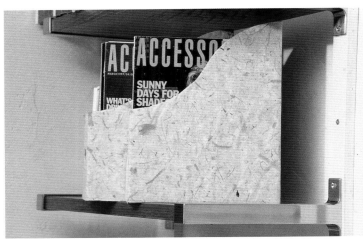

Nepalese-Tibetan-paper covered magazine holders.

Tibetan and Nepalese women make wonderful handmade papers with rich textures. I turned these ordinary, unattractive magazine holders into visually pleasing functional pieces by covering them with handmade paper.

Materials

- Cardboard magazine holders
- Decorative paper (sufficient to cover the magazine holder)
- Multipurpose glue
- Spray adhesive
- Scissors
- Weights (soup cans will work)
- Old newspaper
- Craft knife

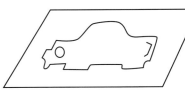

Place magazine holder on paper.

Cut finger holes.

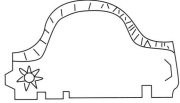

Clip edges of magazine holder to fold.

Instructions

This project is suitable for all skill levels. Cover worktable with newspaper.

1 Place decorative paper right side down (wrong side should face you) on work surface.

2 Fold magazine holder along score lines.

3 Place magazine holder right side down flat on decorative paper, ensuring there is at least 2" of paper around all edges. Place weight on magazine holder.

4 Starting at one side, lift side of magazine holder and spray adhesive lightly and liberally over the surface. Immediately lower side onto decorative paper. Smooth your hand over the entire surface to adhere paper to magazine holder. Repeat process on other sides of magazine holder.

5 Trim around decorative paper leaving 1" of paper around edges of magazine holder.

6 (Skip this step if your magazine holder does not have a finger hole.) Starting at the center of the finger hole, cut away the paper in the finger hole as shown in the illustration. Pull the pieces of paper through to the wrong side of the magazine holder and glue in place. Allow to dry as necessary.

7 Using scissors, clip the 1" paper to the edge of the magazine corner around curved edges. Clipping will allow you to curve the paper around the edges. Pull the paper over to wrong side and glue in place. Allow to dry as necessary.

8 Use craft knife to cut paper in slits where tab fits.

Raffia-wrapped Clay Pot

Raffia-wrapped clay pot.

A raffia-wrapped clay pot makes a great desk accessory.

Materials

- ❒ Unfinished clay planter
- ❒ Raffia (two or more colors)
- ❒ General purpose glue
- ❒ Sponge brush
- ❒ Vinyl gloves
- ❒ Plastic sheeting

Instructions

This project is suitable for all skill levels.

1 Cover work surface with plastic sheeting.

2 Using sponge brush, apply glue about 1/4" way up the side of the clay pot starting from bottom.

3 Wrap raffia around glued-area of planter. Alternate colors to suit your preference.

4 Repeat Steps 2 and 3 until pot is completely wrapped with raffia. Allow to dry.

Proverbs capture the wisdom and experience of a society. As a Sierra Leonean proverb goes:

"Proverbs are the daughters of experience."

In pithy, simple phrases, proverbs share centuries of experience and sage advice that is relevant through the ages:

"A wise man who knows proverbs, reconciles difficulties."
(Yoruba proverb)

The next group of projects incorporates proverbs in fun ways. Here's a small selection of proverbs you could use in your projects. Look for proverbs from your own community and other societies that you may use.

African Proverbs

No matter how long the night, the day is sure to come.
(Democratic Republic of Congo)

He who teaches, learns. (Ethiopia)

When spider webs unite, they can tie up a lion. (Ethiopia)

If you offend, ask for pardon; if offended forgive. (Ethiopia)

Knowledge is like a garden: if it is not cultivated, it cannot be harvested. (Guinea)

Asking questions is never silly.

Elderliness is not a disease, but wealth.

A lie can annihilate a thousand truths.

Wise men are as rare as eagles that fly high in the sky.

Working in the fields is hard, but hunger is harder.

Every stream has its source.

A sandstorm passes; the stars remain.

The heart of an evil person is never pure.

A monkey cannot dare what an elephant can.

Chinese Proverbs

Enjoy yourself. It's later than you think.

Enough shovels of earth-a mountain. Enough pails of water-a river.

A fall into a ditch makes you wiser.

Forget injuries, never forget kindness.

A gem cannot be polished without friction, nor a man perfected without trials.

Govern a family as you would cook a small fish-very gently.

Great souls have wills, feeble ones only have wishes.

A journey of a thousand miles begins with a single step.

Learning is a treasure that will follow its owner everywhere.

Italian Proverbs

How poor is a home without a woman! (Sicilian proverb)

He who finds a friend, finds a treasure.

You never forget your first love.

The tongue has no bone but it breaks bone.

A good wife is the key to a good home.

The first woman you marry is your wife, the second a companion, the third is nonsense.

Clothes don't make the man.

Love rules without rules.

Lies have short legs.

Man proposes but God disposes.

Weddings and spiritual matters are heaven sent. (Sicilian proverb)

Clear agreements make for good friends.

One enemy is too many and a hundred friends aren't enough.

(Sources: *African Proverbs*, Charlotte and Wolf Leslau, Peter Pauper Press, 1985. www.about.com.)

Personal Stationery

Writing paper personalized with Chinese proverb and stamps.

Personalize your writing paper by adding your touches such as stamps and proverbs onto blank sheets. It's a great way to send a personal and thoughtful message to a friend or loved one. I printed a Chinese proverb at the bottom of these sheets and embossed the top corners with stamps of Chinese floral patterns. The result: handsome stationery with a nice message.

Materials

- ❏ Blank sheets of fine writing paper
- ❏ Sheets of paper for practice
- ❏ Computer
- ❏ Stamps (of your choice)
- ❏ Stamp pad
- ❏ Embossing powder
- ❏ Embossing heat tool

Instructions

This project is suitable for all skill levels

1 Using the formatting features of your word processing software, type out a proverb in the desired font in the footer position. (You may also select the header, or lengthwise, along the margins).

2 Using your practice sheets, print copies of your paper until you are happy with the font choice (style and size) and position of your proverb.

3 Print proverbs on sheets of fine writing paper once you are happy with the font and other layout features.

4 Stamp small decorative patterns in the top corners of the sheet.

5 Emboss the stamps with embossing powder and embossing heat tool.

Italian Gilded Tile

Italian gilded tile.

Materials

- ☐ White ceramic tile, 6" x 6"
- ☐ Silver leaf kit
- ☐ Ceramic tile varnish
- ☐ Safety glasses
- ☐ Vinyl gloves
- ☐ Sponge brushes
- ☐ Red paint
- ☐ Paint bush
- ☐ Rinsing water
- ☐ Glue
- ☐ Plastic sheeting

Express beautiful thoughts in elegant style with this simple-to-make project.

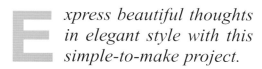

He who finds a friend finds a treasure.

-*Italian Proverb*

Instructions

This project is suitable for all skill levels (minors must be supervised when working with silver leaf). Review manufacturer's instructions for using silver leaf before starting. You may require additional supplies based on manufacturer's instructions.

1 Wash and dry ceramic tile.

2 Cover work surface with plastic sheeting.

3 Photocopy Italian proverb. Tear out the proverb so paper edges surrounding the lettering is uneven.

4 Using light strokes, paint red wash paint over the torn out lettering. Allow to dry.

5 Follow the manufacturer's instructions and apply silver leaf to the ceramic tile. Allow silver leaf to dry.

6 Position and glue the proverb lettering in center of gilded tile. Allow to dry.

7 Seal the surface of the tile with two coats of varnish. Allow to dry between coats.

Pillow Talk

E mbroidered
Silk Pillows.

Materials

- [ ] Yellow dupioni or Thai silk, 1¼ yd
- [ ] Red dupioni or Thai silk, 1 yd
- [ ] 3/8" cord for making piping, 1½ yd
- [ ] Muslin, 1¼ yd
- [ ] Matching yellow sewing thread
- [ ] Matching red sewing thread
- [ ] Pillow filling
- [ ] Pins
- [ ] Scissors
- [ ] Tape measure
- [ ] Ruler
- [ ] Iron
- [ ] Choice of proverb
- [ ] Tracing paper
- [ ] Paper
- [ ] Pencil
- [ ] Computer with word processing software
- [ ] Marking pen or pencil (one that will not leave permanent mark on silk)
- [ ] Programmable embroidery sewing machine
- [ ] Embroidery hoop (if embroidering pillow yourself)
- [ ] Machine embroidery thread (if embroidering pillow yourself)

Instructions

This project requires intermediate sewing skills (making bias tape, covering piping, and stitching piping to pillow fronts). You must have a programmable embroidery machine, or take the pillow front to a commercial shop to be embroidered. Refer to your machine handbook for a list of other supplies needed for embroidery. Disregard this step if a commercial service will embroider your pillow.

1

For front:
Cut one rectangle 20" x 20" out of yellow silk
Cut one rectangle 20" x 20" out of muslin

For back:
Cut two rectangles 8" x 11" out of yellow silk

For piping:
Out of red silk, cut sufficient strips of 2" wide strips to make bias to cover 1-1/2 yd of piping cord

For pillow form:
Cut two rectangles 10" x 11" out of muslin

2 Preparing pillow front for embroidery: Fold front silk and muslin pieces and mark center point on each. Measuring from this center point, measure and mark a rectangle 10" x 11" on the right side of both the silk and muslin.

3 With raw edges even, matching center points, and wrong sides together, pin muslin to pillow front. Baste muslin and silk together just inside the marked rectangle lines. Zigzag raw edges of pillow front to join silk and muslin together. Zigzagging the raw edges will prevent raveling as you handle fabric in next steps.

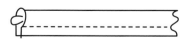

Encase cord piping in silk bias.

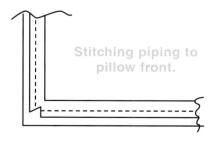

Stitching piping to pillow front.

4 Mark on and cut out of tracing paper a 9" x 10" rectangle to represent your finished pillow front. Using your computer, print out several arrangements of your proverb in several font styles, sizes and colors that you find pleasing. Place the printed proverbs under the tracing paper rectangle and determine which font style, color, and size you prefer. You may need to repeat this process until you are satisfied.

5 Embroidering pillow front: Follow your machine's guidelines for programming your proverb in your selected font size and color. Also follow machine guidelines for preparing your machine and fabric to embroider proverb on pillow. Once set-up is complete, embroider pillow front. Ensure that you center your embroidery around the marked center point.

6 If you are using a commercial service to embroider your pillow fronts, take your pillow front with your final choice of proverb format (Step 3) to your service provider. Clearly indicate the center point and ensure that the service provider centers the embroidery around the marked center point.

7 Preparing pillow front for sewing: Cut out pillow front along the edges of the 11" x 10" rectangle that you marked in Step 1.

8 Preparing pillow back: Along one 11" edge of each piece fold over a ½" seam and press. Fold over and press a second ½" seam, completely encasing the raw edge. Stitch ½" from edge of second fold.

9 Making covered piping: Make bias from 2"-wide red silk strips.

10 Fold bias in half-lengthwise, gently finger press. Encase piping cord inside bias and pin and baste in place so you have ½" seam allowance on either side of piping.

11 Joining bias to pillow front: With raw edges even, starting at the bottom edge, pin piping to pillow front. You will have to clip the piping when you come to the pillow corners so that you can smoothly follow the pillow edges.

12 To join the piping ends smoothly, cut away some of the cord so that the ends meet snugly. Cut bias fabric on each end so it extends 1" beyond cord. Turn under bias edge by ½". Arrange ends so that the folded edges neatly finish piping. Pin ends in place.

13 Baste in place, stitching as close to the piping as you can. Use a zipper foot if you do not have a piping foot.

14 Joining pillow front and back: With right sides together and raw edges even, baste and stitch the pillow back sections to the front using a ½" seam. Note: Back sections will overlap. Trim seam allowance and finish raw edges with zigzag stitch. Turn to right side. Press

15 Making the pillow form: With right sides together and raw edges even, stitch muslin sections together using a ½" seam. Leave a 4" opening along one edge of pillow. Trim seams. Turn to right side. Press.

16 Stuff with pillow filling. Machine or hand-stitch 4" opening to close.

17 Insert pillow form into yellow silk pillow.

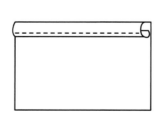

Finishing piping.

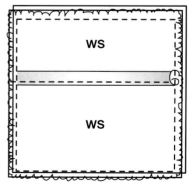

Joining pillow front and back.

Burnt Orange Silk Pillow (16"-16")

Materials

- ❏ Burnt orange dupioni or Thai silk, 1¼ yd
- ❏ Gold decorative trim, 2 yd
- ❏ Muslin, 1 yd
- ❏ Matching sewing thread
- ❏ Pillow form, 16" x 16"
- ❏ Pins
- ❏ Scissors
- ❏ Ruler
- ❏ Tape measure
- ❏ Iron
- ❏ Choice of proverb
- ❏ Tracing paper
- ❏ Paper
- ❏ Computer
- ❏ Pencil
- ❏ Marking pen or pencil (one that will not leave permanent mark on silk)
- ❏ Embroidery hoop (if embroidering pillow yourself)
- ❏ Machine embroidery thread (if embroidering pillow yourself)

Instructions

1 **For front:**
Cut one square, 20" x 20", out of silk
Cut one square, 20" x 20", out of muslin

For back:
Cut two rectangles, 10" x 17", out of yellow silk

2 Preparing pillow front for embroidery: Fold front silk and muslin rectangles and mark center point on each. Measuring from this center point, measure and mark a square 17" x 17" on the right side of both the silk and muslin.

3 Follow Steps 2 through 4 for the Yellow Silk Pillow to complete pillow front.

4 Preparing pillow front for sewing: Cut out pillow front along the edges of the 17" x 17" rectangle that you marked in Step 16 for the Yellow Silk Pillow.

5 Preparing pillow back: Along one 17" edge of each piece fold over a ½" seam and press. Fold over and press a second ½" seam, completely encasing the raw edge. Stitch ½" from edge of second fold.

6 Joining pillow front and back: Follow Step 12 above.

A journey of a thou...
begins with a sing

he moon is not full, the stars
hine more brightly.

He who teache.

9 | Clothing

Stamping and stenciling are great techniques for adding your personal style to your wardrobe. If you sew, make your own fabric with stamps and stencils of your choice. Then make your one-of-a-kind fashions and home furnishings with your unique fabric. Don't sew? You can add your design touches to purchased garments; T-shirts or simple blouses. Once you are comfortable with stamping and stenciling simple garments, add your touch to other garments such as skirts, dresses, pants, or coats.

Here are a few ideas you can consider using to personalize your garments.

Silk chiffon blouse.

Mehndi Silk Chiffon Blouse

Silk chiffon blouse.

I loved this Oscar de la Renta blouse (Vogue pattern 2712). To make mine special, I stenciled delicate Mehndi designs onto each layer of ruffles. The result is a sophisticated blouse. Team it with a black silk chiffon skirt, and *voilà*—it's an elegant outfit.

Interestingly, I used the "Bakari Santos Series" of stencils available from Lakaye Studio, a Mehndi center, to decorate this blouse. Instead of using the stencils for body art, as would be done at Lakaye, I used them for decorating my wardrobe. Look for stencils from unusual places when you design and plan projects.

Nomad Coat–Fusion of Cultures

Nomad coat.
Design: Ronke
Luke-Boone.

Thai, African, and Hopi blend seamlessly in this Nomad coat (Hibiscus™ 1003). Thai silk borders and cuffs offset the greens and purples in the African cottons used in the coat. Hopi motifs stenciled in gold on the cuffs add sparkle to the coat. It's a great cover-up for evening and cocktail wear.

Linen Kuba–patterned Outfit

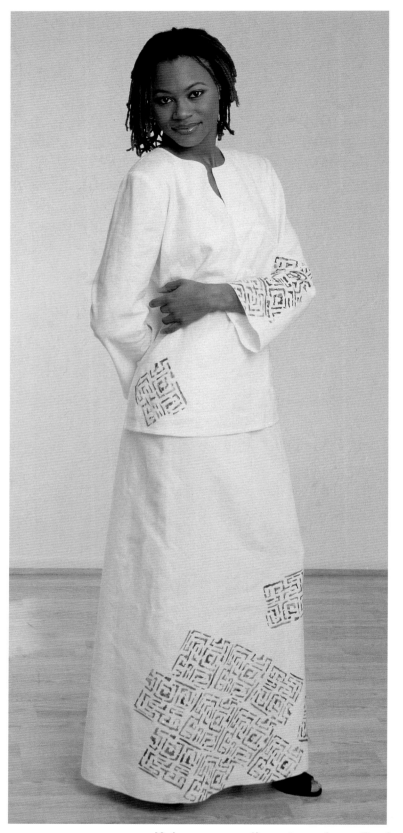

Here's another example of using stencils to add pizzazz to an outfit. To decorate this linen two-piece outfit, I used a stencil inspired by Kuba cloth patterns to add color and interest to a simple outfit. This is the same stencil I used to etch the elegant glass container shown earlier in this book. Same stencil, different looks. The result is an elegant summer outfit with timeless appeal.

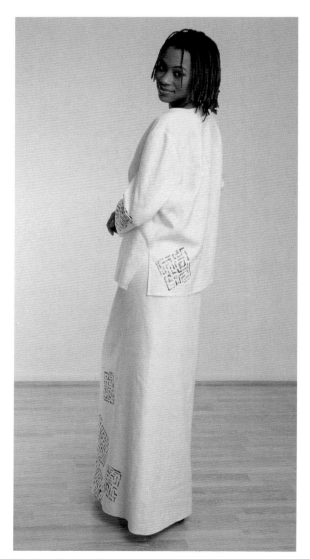

Kuba summer linen two-piece. Design: Ronke Luke-Boone.

Ibo Water Spirit Dress

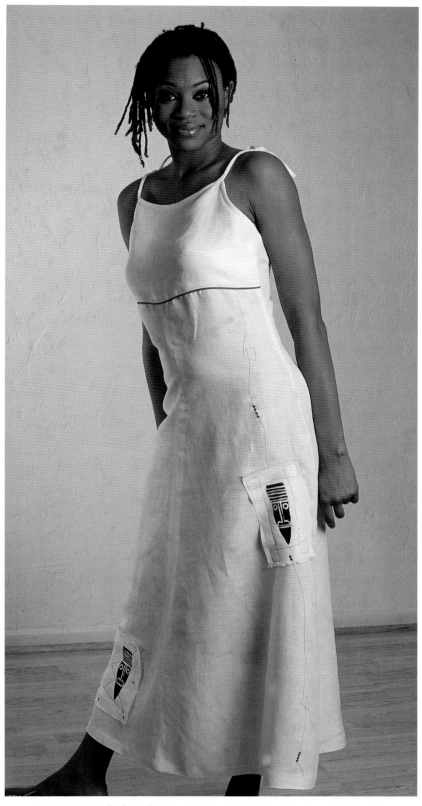

Ibo Water Spirit linen dress. Design: Ronke Luke-Boone.

You don't need much to add visual interest. Stencils of the Ibo Water Spirit add an ethnic twist to this sleek, white linen summer dress. It was a favorite of mine last summer. I stenciled the images of the Water Spirit onto rectangle linen patches and stitched them onto the dress with red embroidery thread. (I obtained the image of the Ibo Water Spirit from African Designs from Traditional Sources. See resources, page 125).

Linen and Korhogo Jacket

T he Ibo Water Spirit adds interest to the back of this linen, Korhogo cloth, and mudcloth jacket.

A stylish jacket out of linen, Korhogo cloth, and mudcloth. Design: Ronke Luke-Boone.

Ibo Water Spirit adds interest to the back of the jacket.

Indian-inspired Summer Sheath

Indian summer sheath. Design: Ronke Luke-Boone.

Blue jewel tones and tiny straps conjure up dreams of warm tropical places, but I transformed them into an exotic sheath by stenciling the mid section with an Indian-inspired floral pattern. Curls and swirls of pretty buds and vines in rich yellows, greens, and blues add drama.

Mehndi Linen Blouse

Mehndi linen blouse.

I put my special stamp on this purchased linen blouse by stenciling a Mehndi pattern on the borders and hem. This is a simple way to create interesting elements on your blouses. (I used the "Bakari Santos Series" of stencils available from Lakaye Studio for this project).

Mudcloth T-shirt

Mudcloth T-shirt.

I screen-printed a mudcloth pattern on plain white T-shirts. Try the same idea using stencils or screen-printing.

Bibliography

Publications

Baquedano, Elizabeth. *Aztec Inca & Maya. Discovering the Mysterious World of these Ancient Peoples-Their beliefs, rituals, and fascinating civilizations*. New York: Alfred A. Knopf, 1993.

Bassman, Theda. *Treasures of the Hopi*. Flagstaff, AZ: Northland Publishing, 1997.

Caruana, Wally. *Aboriginal Art*. New York: Thames & Hudson, 1993.

D'Amato, Janet and Alex. *Native American Craft Inspirations*. New York: M. Evans & Company, Inc., 1992.

Dawson, Imogen. *Clothes & Crafts in Aztec Times*. Dillon Press, 1997.

Day, Lewis F. *Pattern Design*. New York: Dover Press, 1999.

Elliot, Marion. *The Tile Decorating Book, Decorating and Hand-painting Tiles-A Practical Guide*. Lorenz Books, 1997.

Fabius, Carine. *Mehndi*. New York: Three Rivers Press, 1998.

Leslau, Charlotte and Wolf. *African Proverbs*. Mount Vernon: Peter Pauper Press, 1985.

Luke-Boone, Ronke. *African Fabrics, Sewing Contemporary Fashion with Ethnic Flair*. Iola, WI: Krause, 2001

Parker, Mary S. *Sashiko, Easy and Elegant Japanese Designs for Decorative Machine Embroidery*. Asheville, NC: Lark Books, 1999.

Seward, Pat. *Cultures of the World, Morocco*. 2nd ed. Tarrytown, NY: Benchmark Books, 1995.

Stribling, Mary Lou. *Crafts from North American Indian Arts. Techniques, Designs and Contemporary Applications*. New York: Crown Publishers Inc., 1975.

Willis, W. Bruce. *The Adinkra Dictionary*. Washington, D.C.: The Pyramid Complex, 1998.

Ofori-Ansa, Dr. Kwaku. *Adinkra Wall Poster*. Maryland: Sankofa Publications.

Web Sites

"About Mingei,"
http://www.blueandwhiteamerica.com/Mingei.html

"Aboriginal Art Online,"
http://www.Aboriginalartonline.com

"Aboriginal Australia,"
http://www.Aboriginalaustralia.com

"About the Hopi Indians,"
http://www.3mesas.com/hopi/main.html

"Henna and the Moroccan Aesthetic,"
Lisa Butterworth, http://www.kenzi.com

"Hopi Indians,"
http://inkido.indiana.edu/w310work/romac/hopi.htm

"Jinta Desert Art,"
http://www.jintaart.com.au

"Kuwawata, Welcome to the Official Site of the Hopi Tribe,"
http://www.hopi.nsn.us/

"Logoi.com-The Online Language Source,"
http://www.logoi.com/

"Piet Mondriaan,"
www.the-artfile.com/uk/artists/mondriaan/mondriaan.htm

"Piet Mondrian Online,"
www.artcyclopedia.com/artists/mondrian_piet.html

"Piet Mondrian,"
http://www.guggenheimcollection.org/site/artist_bio_112.html

"Piet Mondrian,"
http://titan.glo.be/~gd30144/mondrian.html

"A Rambling Romp through Tulip History,"
http://www.bulb.com

Resources

Acrylic Paint
Nova Color®
Artex Manufacturing Company
5894 Blackwelder St.
Culver City, CA 90232
(310) 838-2094
Offers wide selection of paints for
 stamping and stenciling.

Adinkra Symbols
Education Resources
Adinkra Wall Chart
Sankofa Publications
Contact: Dr. Kwaku Ofori-Ansa
Associate Professor of Art, Howard University
2211 Amherst Rd.
Hyattsville, MD 20783
(202) 806-7075
A great poster with Adinkra designs and their
meanings.
Dr. Ofori-Ansa is also available for lectures.

African Designs
Williams, Geoffrey. African Designs from Traditional
Sources. New York: Dover Publications, 1971.
Excellent resource for designs from across Africa.

Australian Aboriginal Art & History
Aboriginal Australia Culture Centre
86 Todd Street
Alice Springs, NT 0870
AUSTRALIA
Tel: +61 (8) 89 52 34 08
Fax: +61 (8) 89 53 26 78

Contact® Paper
Home hardware supply stores.

Hopi History & Culture
Hopi Cultural Preservation Office
(928) 734-3610
Fax: (928) 734-3629

HOPI (Hopi Office of Public Information)
P.O. Box 123
Kykotsmovi, AZ 86039
(928) 734-3283
Fax: (928) 734-6648

Lampshades and Supplies
100 Gray Rd.
Falmouth, ME 04105
Fax: (800) 554-1755
http://www.mainelyshades.com

Mehndi and Henna Traditions
Lakaye Studio
Contact: Carine Fabius
1800 N. Highland Ave.
Ste 316
Hollywood, CA 90028
www.earthhenna.com
Offers stencils and supplies for Mehndi and
henna body painting.

Maison Kenzi
Contact: Lisa Butterworth
(718) 789-1545
http://www.kenzi.com/
Offers henna kit and henna body art services.
Web site offers good primer on henna
traditions in Morocco.

Mingei
Mingeikan-The Japan Folk Crafts Museum
http://www.Mingeikan.or.jp/Pages/entrance-e.html

Mingei International Museum
1439 El Prado
Balboa Park
San Diego, CA 92101
http://www.Mingei.org

Peabody Essex Museum, Salem, Massachusetts
Seattle Art Museum, Seattle, Washington
Cleveland Museum of Art, Cleveland, Ohio
Brooklyn Museum of Art, Brooklyn, New York

Patterns
Nomad Coat (Hibiscus™ 1003) available from:
R.L. Boone
P.O. Box 3276
Falls Church, VA 22043
(703) 448-3884
Email: info@rlboone.com
www.rlboone.com

Sashiko
Textile Museum
2320 S Street, NW
Washington, D. C. 20008-4088
(202) 667-0441
www.textilemuseum.org

Index

Aboriginal symbols 25
Adinkra symbols 37
Adire 53
Apache 82
Apache basket 82
Australian Aboriginal Art 25
Aztec-Inca-Maya 23

Bamboo 84

Chinese 86
Chinese calligraphy 89
Cutting Stencils 9

Great Hunting Scene 43

Henna motifs 45
Hopi 44, 55

Ibo 119
India 100
Islamic and Arabic tiles 94

Japan 63

Kashmir 100
Kente 39
Korhogo cloth 48

Kuba cloth 33, 67

Mehndi-Henna 45
Mingei 63
Moroccan tile patterns 57
Mudcloth 40

Nigeria 53

Paisley 97, 100
Piet Mondrian 70
Proverbs 108

Rock paintings 34

Sashiko 65
Seminole 102
Shoji 87
Stenciling 12

Tulips 29

Yoruba 53

Display your HERITAGE WITH Pride

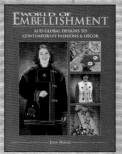

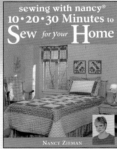